Education
for the Twenty-First
Century

William H. Boyer

Education for the Twenty-First Century

William H. Boyer

Published by Caddo Gap Press
3145 Geary Boulevard PMB 275
San Francisco, California 94118 U.S.A.

ISBN 1-880192-38-1

Price - $24.95

Printed on recycled paper.

Library of Congress Cataloging-in-Publication Data

Boyer, William H. (William Harrison), 1924-
    Education for the twenty-first century / William H. Boyer.
        p. cm.
    Includes bibliographical references
    ISBN 1-880192-38-1 (alk. paper)
    1. Education--Social aspects--United States. 2. Education--Aims and
objectives--United States. 3. Peace--Study and teaching. 4. Critical pedagogy. I. Title.

LC191.8.U6 B69 2002
370'.973--dc21

                                                        2001043825

Contents

Section Two: Critiques of Education

Section Four: Glossary and Sources

Dedication

This book is dedicated to Theodore Brameld, the leading philosopher of educational reconstruction in the 20th Century.

Introduction

When Ted Brameld's *Education as Power* was republished by Caddo Gap Press in the fall of 2001, I was encouraged to follow up with my professional essays and articles that address other issues of reconstructionist educational philosophy. Ted Brameld had greatly influenced my thought as a graduate student with his *Patterns of Educational Philosophy*. He later became a colleague and close friend and we shared new ideas. At that time I was pioneering futures education, world order education, and ecological education. Ted was interested in all of these fields.

This book consists of most of my journal articles written and published over the past three decades, a period during which I was also the author of three books—*Education for Annihilation, Alternative Futures: Designing Social Change*, and *Americas Future: Transition to the 21st Century*. These articles and books show how to get beyond the war system, the poverty system, and the ecocide system. With these writings I was seeking to establish political and economic foundations of education, disciplines that had been largely ignored, even though educators had often used "democracy" as their overriding principle and goal.

My primary academic background is in philosophy but I had also taught in the field of psychology, and it was apparent to me that a root flaw in teacher education is the attempt to use psychology as the basis for educational philosophy. This fatal error persists. Psychology deals with "how," not with "what." Professors of education need to know more about economics, politics, and ecology to help students control the beliefs and mythologies that drive institutions. Instead, education is too often built on technique such as computer skills, while the big questions about alternative futures are never asked.

Most education is aimed at fitting people into existing institutions, but since our institutions have often become obsolete or even pathological, education should not be used to perpetuate them. Rather, education should be the basis for helping provide power to people to reconstruct institutions so that they are more democratic.

Survival requires knowledge which helps us move beyond the institutionalization of the systems of war, poverty, and ecological destruction. We need a new kind of citizenship in the Twenty-First Century. Training young people to adjust to corporations is not citizenship education. People need to learn to design the world of the future, one in which institutions serve people. Nations and corporations controlled the Twentieth Century and are heading us toward global warming, increased poverty, and nuclear war. Instead of planning for a sustainable high quality of life, we have used growth economics and GNP as the engines that direct our future.

The United States is providing the wrong model to the world, based on continuation of the Twentieth Century growth model in which national power and global corporations rule the world. If we are to have democracy rather than corporate control, people will need to learn to design a just and sustainable future, so in addition to new politics a new education will be needed.

These are the concerns that underlie the articles in this book. Hopefully, they will be used in teacher education and fields such as political science and futures studies to illuminate alternatives to the direction we are now headed. Some repetition of basic ideas resulted inevitably from applying a consistent theory to the themes of each article.

The articles were written over a thirty-year period and a close examination will reveal how few of the basic issues have yet been confronted.

The articles are arranged so that they should be especially useful in seminars where each article can be analyzed and discussed. Their reproduction does not require permission, provided their use is not for profit and credit is given.

Introduction
to Section One

Goals of Education

Section One focuses on the goals of education, which includes knowledge necessary to be an effective citizen in the Twenty-First Century. A central question for all educators is: What knowledge is of most importance?

The answer must take account of this period of history—where the world is and where it is going. Then judgements must be made about whether policies and institutions are contributing to social justice and human survival or to poverty, injustice, and ecological degradation.

Such education is both scientific and ethical. It requires commitment to the worth and dignity of people now and in the future. It obligates us to use democratic processes to create a future that serves such ethical goals. It helps empower people to participate in creating a just society which also respects the ecological life support system on which all future generations depend.

Chapter One

Boyer's Conception of Reconstructionism:
Old Order/New Order

*Education should help people participate
in changing obsolete institutions
so those institutions become more just and sustainable.*

I share with Ted Brameld the assumption that what is worthy of being called "education" helps give people power to participate in social change rather than merely fitting into the existing social order. Ted used his background in philosophy and anthropology to focus on "culture." Working within the same general framework, I focus instead on political planning. I also begin with the assumption that most institutions are obsolete because they are pre-ecological and pre-ethical. As a result, I assume we now live in what I call the "upside-down society."

The central goal of education is then to help correct obsolete institutions—to move from one era to another—from one based on economic expansion to one centered on ecological and ethical principles.

This requires macro-priorities which define where we are and where we need to go.

From the Upside-Down Society

From Current Nonsustainable Present (priorities):

1. Economics
2. Social Needs
3. Ecology

To Sustainable Future (priorities):

1. Ecology
2. Social Needs
3. Economics

The overall priority now driving change and policy is Economics. Social effect of economic forces is given consideration as a second priority, and ecological considerations are last.

Macro-Priorities

Using macro-priorities permits any group to see what the order should be:

1. Ecology should be first, for the biological life-support system is a pre-requisite to everything else.

2. Social Needs are next in an ethics-based future.

3. Economics can then be free to expand markets and make profits and follow people's wants, within the above constraints, but human needs have priority. Economic activity is then subject to limits because there are other priorities which serve present and future generations.

Given the essential elements of these two "orders," the basic role of education is clear: to help people participate in social change moving from the old order to the new one.

These macro-priorities of the future are not arbitrary but the result of two considerations: (1) The advancement of science into ecology which connects ecology with human survival; and (2) The use of the essential ethical principle in democracy: "the worth and dignity of the human being." Given this ethical premise, any institution can be evaluated by its contribution to human needs and human quality of life. Indicators can measure institutional success and therefore social progress.

Ethics-Centered Education

Ted Brameld was criticized for his concept of "defensible partiality," which was a way of defending the need for a justifiable bias. Critics presumed bias meant that education would consist of propaganda and indoctrination. They thought that to be objective required neutrality.

Ted saw the need for value presuppositions, and defended defensible partiality if it was grounded on an "open, unrestricted criticism and comparison," supported even "after the defense occurs" (*Patterns of Educational Philosophy*, p. 473).

I agree with Ted that "objectivity" involves accuracy and not neutrality but I also want the selection of accurate information which focuses on the way political conditions bear on "the worth and dignity of people." This is a radical human rights position, which shifts from democracy as only process to the substantive side of democracy. Processes and means should serve ethical goals and institutions should be reinvented if they do not serve people.

Neutrality is then unethical when it means indifference. (Could we be neutral to the Holocaust?) But in the same way that we do not advocate a school of public sickness to "balance" a school of public health in a university so we must make sure that education uses ethical principles to determine the inevitable selectivity of subject matter. If we are "for" the "worth and dignity of the human person" we are also for human rights and against human exploitation.

Ethical principles are determined *a-priori*, though their application is contextual. What is needed in the design of institutions is ethical analysis of institutions. How does "free trade" bear on the worth and dignity of people? Are people then commodities to be priced by and traded by the market?

Students get their real power by learning to focus on solutions to the change of institutions and policies which now cause unfairness to people. For instance, foreign policy that serves only national self-interest becomes categorically unethical. Most social science textbooks fail, on the basis of this rationale, to meet defensible "educational" standards. They often treat nation-state domination descriptively as though the data were dealing with natural science subject matter instead of people and their lives.

Ideology Traps

Transition from the old upside-down society requires understanding of the belief systems that undermine people's capacity to reinvent institutions appropriate to this period of history.

Ideologies endemic to the culture are the main obstacles. They paralyze the capacity of students to become a history creator, for they are based on dogmatic belief. In the same way that fundamentalist religion provides absolutism rather than critical thinking, so does ideology—it consists of secular fundamentalism.

Examples are beliefs that:

1. Capitalism and market economics are the basis for democracy.

2. Local control is always best.

3. Property rights are inviolable.

4. Natural resources should be allocated through market economics.

5. World order should be based on national military power.

6. Gross National Product (GNP) is the best indicator of progress.

7. Technology is the foundation of GNP.

8. Competition will produce a just distribution of wealth and income.

Such assumptions need to be treated as cultural beliefs by which students can test their ethical and ecological implications against alternatives. Teachers need to assume that they must take students from their normal miseducation of induction in the old order and move them toward more power to re-examine their culture and its institutions. Some beliefs liberate—some enslave. The real institutional games may be like the parlor game of Monopoly in which some people are pre-committed to either total wealth or absolute poverty, merely by playing the game. Conventional education tells them to learn to compete more efficiently and join as a player. Reconstruction education helps them consider whether they are playing the wrong game and if so to design a better one. The rules determine the outcome. If the outcome is unethical the rules should be changed. The current dominant economic game contributes to our economic oligarchy and undermines democracy. The result is anti-ecological and lacking in social ethics. The upside-down society in which we live lacks social goals and is driven by short-range, reactive *ad hoc* accommodations to crises. Schools should be teaching people to be involved in long-range planning based on sustainable ecosystems and human needs.

By the time students have completed high school they should have some understanding of local and state political issues and have some experience participating in them.

The school must greatly widen the sources of material from the conventional mass media and mainstream textbooks into the nonpopular media. Conventional mass media is a propaganda trap from which few citizens escape. The result is to reinforce the political power of a nation that along with multinationals is dominating poor nations and exploiting their people and resources. The global oligarchy is dependent on widespread ignorance perpetuated by the dominant world nation—the United States. Self-righteous nationalism, reinforced by most schools, keeps the systems intact.

Students need to have some knowledge of alternative futures, especially as they relate to employment so they can contribute to the design of a future society that offers opportunity for everyone to be employed. People are now victims of a particular conception of capitalist economics that includes compulsory unemployment for 5 or 6 percent, which is double and triple for youth and minorities. People are treated as commodities to be bought and sold. No future is promising which continues this unnecessary violation of basic human rights to employment at a living wage. Unemployment exists because people tolerate it. They tolerate it because they see no alternative. They see no alternative because schools and mass media rarely focus on solutions.

Computer skills and mathematical skills should be connected to problems that serve the public interest rather than only to the competitive efficiency of corporations. These skills will then be useful in a variety of roles later on, including jobs. The misemphasis in current education is in treating schools merely as technical education and disconnected fields of knowledge to fit students into obsolete but dominant institutions. This makes much current education part of the problem. Even what is called economic education is usually capitalist economics rather than ecological-ethics-centered economics. Good economic material is available but out of the mainstream. The overall priority of conventional economics is the insidious driving force that produces the "upside-down" society.

Communities as Laboratories

Students need to be involved in investigations of their community with respect to water and air quality. "Carrying capacity" and "quality of life" need to be given operational meaning and the way future generations are impacted under current land use and resource needs to illuminate how structural exploitation of the common heritage consists of stealing from future generations. This leads to connections between public policy, institutional ethics, and ecology.

The job of the school should be to help people have control over their institutions and therefore their common future, else what meaning is there to democracy? They now have little or none, because education of all kinds focuses on providing information and skills to fit them into the current upside-down world. Communities are driven by an economic growth mania in which people have virtually no control.

Current government based on constituency politics provides a system of band-aid reaction to crisis but no real long-range goals. Our state and federal constitutions need to include long-range goals created by public initiatives (direct democracy). It is time to vote for goals, not merely for people, so that those people we do vote for will know what they are supposed to do. We are now the goal-less society, not knowing where we are going but being busily involved in getting there.

Education and the Future

One of Ted Brameld's most useful books was *Education as Power.* With more attention to the redesign of political and economic systems, students can be citizens in the 21st century who have the power to help create a more sustainable and just future. Current education generally makes students irrelevant and insignificant because the kind of power that would help them guide the future is out of their reach. A different kind of education is vitally needed in which political power is shifted to people and democracy is revitalized.

There is nothing strange or even "radical" about such a philosophy; it is merely citizenship education for democracy in this period of human history. It turns citizens into planners and provides recognition of a basic fact—there is no alternative to planning, only who will plan and for what goals. Nations, corporations, and the military are now the key planners. Schools either will help the public be the key players in defining the future or the future will continue to serve the dangerous, unethical, and unsustainable institutions that now create the future.

References

Brameld, T. (1965). *Education As Power*. New York: Holt, Rinehart, & Winston. Republished in 2000 for The Society for Educational Reconstruction by Caddo Gap Press, San Francisco, CA.

Brameld, T. (1971). *Patterns of Educational Philosophy: Divergence and Convergence in Culturological Perspective*. New York: Holt, Rinehart, & Winston.

Chapter Two

Creativity Type II:
Designing and Creating World Futures

*There is nothing in human potentiality
to prevent us learning to transform
institutions so they serve people.*

A common educational error has been to assume that children are naturally creative and that it is good for them to express their natural creativity, whatever the results. This permits moral anarchy by default, for it ignores the ends that creativity can serve. Thieves, exploiters, and various types of murderers may be very creative, but we may wish they were less so. Unless creativity is instrumental to life-affirming goals it can serve pathological ends.

"Creativity" has various meanings; it can refer to a contribution to society or anything new to the person who is creating. It may refer to creative processes or to creative products. The fine arts provide only one of a variety of creative processes; science, when it is not the cookbook type, may be equally creative. Any art, when it is formula art, may be quite uncreative.

When creativity is defined through the narrow perspective of western individualism, it ignores the synergistic effect of group interaction. "Democracy" need not be merely an election technique;

it can be a philosophy of group creativity. If groups can create social change, and if the size of the groups and the scope of the process can be enlarged, we have the prospect of an unprecedented but crucially needed form of creative behavior where *people join collectively to guide the course of history.* The rest of this paper will focus on this expanded conception of creative action in which (1) We create the process by which we can create the future, and (2) We design preferred futures and produce change toward their realization.

I

To apply design to the world's future suggests a task that may first appear ludicrous, arrogant, and impossible. Any design task may appear too great at first, whether it be designing furniture, a house, a landscape, a city, or a new society. Yet isn't it really more startling to continue to assume that the future of the human race should continue to be accidental? Though we recognize that the human race is the dominant species to inhabit this planet and we are increasingly aware that we have the potentiality for reshaping the course of history, we ordinarily assume, however, that history must continue to be either unpredictable or subject to forces beyond human control. We teach ourselves to settle for being either a *spectator* or an *anticipator*, but not a *participator*. We seldom see that the role we have accepted in fact determines how the future is going to be created.

There is an enormous range of devices used by people to convince themselves of their impotence, and an enormous variety of compensatory mechanism—driving big cars, making loud noises with motorcycles, building huge buildings, dropping big bombs—which provide the illusion of power. These compensatory games distract from an analysis of basic social power, which creates the future by directing the dynamics of change. Those who have special advantages under the existing order have a stake in the perpetuation of the mythologies of fatalism, pessimism, and impotence. The existing order is also sustained by ignorance of the way social and natural systems affect human life and by the failure to examine alternative futures.

The dynamics of current change is based primarily on three factors: quantitative expansion of numbers of people, increases in applied knowledge and technology, and a hierarchical system of power within and between nations. This maldistribution of power produces a maldistribution of wealth and income which perpetuates the widening gap between the rich and the poor. The gap is exacerbated both by differential birth levels and by exponentially increasing consumption levels in the rich nations. Projections of resource consumption trends and their pollution by-products provides virtually certain global ecocide within a relatively short length of time, twenty-five to fifty years. Economic inequality lays the groundwork for counter violence. The inequality is itself a form of violence, for the advanced industrial nations gorge themselves in an orgy of overconsumption of the nonrenewable resources that constitutes a common heritage of the entire human race. Meanwhile half the world lives in abject poverty.

"Adjustment" and "adaptation" have been interpreted by virtually all institutions, including the schools, to mean that the individual should adapt to trends. "Adaptation" has, in the double-speak of *1984,* become a way of reinforcing suicidal trends, which leads to Malthusian positive checks. Stability eventually takes place through starvation, predation, and disease. Either the species plans or nature plans. There is no other alternative.

Social planning is radically multilateral. Schools emphasize *individual* planning, if they teach any planning whatsoever. The parable cited by Garrett Hardin in the well-known article, "The Tragedy of the Commons," points out the basic fallacy of individual or unilateral planning, as a central planning strategy. As the story goes, each of a small number of farmers grazed a cow on the commons, providing subsistence for their families. Then one farmer decided to maximize his advantage by getting another cow, and the others did the same to compete. As this process continued, the commons was soon overgrazed and all the cows died. This is a parable of the group in relation to finite resources and it is basic to species planning on planet earth. The *absence* of a structure for multilateral planning within nations and between nations predetermines a global tragedy of the common resources of the planet. The alternative should be clear.

Unless students consider the dynamics of change and make systemic analysis of the components of change, they do not have the "basics" for a better future or even for species survival. Education must not fragment and atomize; it must integrate. Disconnected fragments of information and separate intellectual skills are merely grist for the present techno-structure. Students should study macro-systems, macro-ecology, macroeconomics, and macro-politics. Unless they are helped to develop a world perspective focusing on the structures that sustain life and will determine the quality of life in the future, they are being distracted from the kind of education they need, processed by the system to play out the tragedy of the cows on the commons.

Designing the future requires not only knowledge of baseline trends but also models of preferred futures. It requires models of collective rather than individual preferred futures, for reasons previously stated. Here we shift from science to aspirational *values*. We become artists . As we imagine a preferred future, stimulated by the imagination of others, we then must make compromises between what we consider *desirable* and what is *possible*. If we can also provide the rudiments for a strategy of transition—how to move from here to there—we have the outline for a proposal for social change.

Another tradition of the schools is likely to be an obstacle at this point. The design of futures might be a tolerable violation of sacred pedagogical traditions, but the creation and the testing of the model is likely to be fundamental sacrilege. Yet social action is the means of learning the attitudes and skills that enable us to achieve social goals. The separation of theory from practice is merely one way in which schools preserve the status quo. Under the traditions of mind-body dualism students are taught to disconnect means from ends, thought from emotions. Why should we want to design futures if we do not also increase our power to help realize those goals?

All this is merely another way of talking about relevant citizenship, a topic remarkably obscured by those who say the school should not be political. They fail to distinguish between partisan politics and the "polis" in its generic sense. It is precisely the involvement in community which is central to an education that is humanistic and morally committed. Moral neutrality permits a person to be merely a technician. The problems of common survival, human equality, and environmental quality are not examples of partisan politics, but they are not merely neutral. Unless schools use intellectual processes as instruments to serve world interest goals they will continue to invert means and ends, providing either distraction from basic common problems or teaching intellectual technique to serve an economy already out of control.

II

Students should be taught to analyze current planning processes. Most governmental corporate planning is based on the assumption that we should anticipate trends and then use technology to adjust to the trends. Power companies are predicting a hundred percent increase in energy consumption within ten years. They urge appropriate political and economic response, so that when they build the new power plants (at whatever price to pollution and the world's resources) they can reinforce rising consumption levels and in ten years show that they are prophets and saviors who have confirmed their prediction. Unless futurists understand the role of self-fulfilling prophecies they are part futurist and part menace—primarily the latter.

Most of the ways in which futures are now being created may appear Machiavellian to the spectator. The elite actors on the stage of history appear to have a wide range of alternatives, choosing so often to retain a conspiracy of power against the trapped audience. But Devil theories provide the easy explanation, useful not merely to American presidents but to other moral determinists. It is far more likely that those decision makers who have the power to create history are as much a victim of the mythologies that lock them into the past as are the majorities who are affected by the decision. Myth and ignorance provide the cohesion and stability for the present world order. The schools are a major perpetuator of the selective ignorance which once was called the essential wisdom. What passes for truth in one period can be the plan for suicide in the next.

For example, nationalism has been the secular religion of the Twentieth Century and is still on the upswing in newly developing countries. In the pre-atomic, pre-ecological world of the early twentieth century, nationalism was an integrating force. Whatever one's tribe, the nation melted him into a national, either by democratic or totalitarian means. The significant point is that the world is really one ecologically; it has a life-support system that knows no national boundaries. And if the world is to be one morally, it can have no national boundaries on social justice.

The world has been and will continue to be one ecology. It is not yet one social-moral-political system operating under common law. Unless the political order can plan with respect for the world's ecological life-support system, man will have his nationalism at the price of extinction.

Now in the atomic age, national defense is no longer possible, yet nations cling to an old system which is called national defense but actually is a mutual annihilation system. "Defense" is created by semantics, and "anti-ballistic missile systems" are developed which meet the semantic requirement though not the performance requirement. Such symbolic madness occurs because people are habituated to technological solutions rather than to change of political systems.

But there is nothing in human potentiality to prevent us learning to transform social institutions so that they serve man. Man has been taught to serve his institutions, a cruel irony of history, based on the common sociological principle that means tend to become ends. Again we have a task for education.

Education should devise a new conception of human development, retaining the principle that learning must begin where the child is experientially. Therefore planning-education for first graders will probably take account only of the classroom or the school ground environment. Children may redesign the walls of their classroom. Additional growth (Type II) in the student's experience should permit him to be involved in regional and even state planning by the time he is in high school. As the circle of experience moves outward, it will be seen that local planning cannot occur independent of global planning. Plan Ontario without planning Canada and you have misplanned. Plan Canada without coordinated world planning and you've fiddled while the world prepares to burn.

But world planning is risky business. What about the danger of totalitarian control? Wouldn't we avoid a global 1984 by pursuing the policy of "the best government is the least government"?

This is a small planet with an expanding technology and an increasingly vulnerable biosphere. Transnational organizations are developing rapidly, and common means for managing a world economy and international violence increasingly are seen to be necessary, with pilot models developing rapidly through regional organizations such as the European Common Market. Since world authority is inevitable, the only question is whether it will occur before or after global collapse such as World War III or global ecocide. Therefore the question is not really whether world authority will develop but *when* and *how*, serving what *ends*, by what means of what system of *control*.

Change under the present "system" of nonworld-order occurs primarily by reinforcing random and accidental dynamics of change. This process is exemplified by the schools which have their main effect on the future by *not* teaching planning. If you do not teach students to be involved in social planning, you reinforce the dynamics of existing systems by default. It is an implicit rather than an explicit philosophy of education, which reinforces the status quo.

History is made by what we do and what we fail to do. Schools should be evaluated on the basis of their response to the problems of the world, and we need a theory of identifying the basic problems. If we continue to believe, as some power companies do, that economic trends are inevitable therefore good, schools will continue to provide intellectual skills to help individuals add to efficiency of existing economic systems and will be rewarded for doing so. If people are not taught to examine alternative futures and to select and realize the most morally responsible future, the forces of technology, market place economics, and hierarchical power will lock in existing trends.

It is important to recognize that we cannot actually predict a particular future. Scenarios of alternative futures, such as those in *The Limits of Growth*, are hypotheses. Hypotheses are "if so, then so" relationships. History is a set of causal connections but man can change and initiate new causes. The reason it so often seems that we can predict the future is that we do not change the "if so" conditions. When the conventional inputs occur, the expected results take place. But we have the choice of retaining or altering inputs.

Nothing is more influential in creating a false sense of inevitability than the belief in *determinism,* which causes us either to reinforce directly the existing dynamics of history or to do nothing and reinforce them by default. Alienation and identity crises are largely byproducts of social systems that obstruct the development of community. A pathological social structure produces alienation, anomie, and depoliticization, which feeds back to perpetuate the social structure and locks in the system. Education should be an instrument for breaking the cycle, but its mode of analysis has been too psychological, too pre-committed to a belief that the disease is in the patient. Counseling and guidance has usually been a band-aid operation for individual symptoms, adjusting the individual to the system, exacerbating the social pathology.

Futurist education should not be an escape from the present. Quite the opposite, it should be a way of deciding what is really worth doing *now* by deciding where the action should lead. It is presentism that consists of romantic escape, for it ignores the reality of time. One's life should balance both *being* and *doing,* but if one is doing something significant the two processes are combined.

The reason for planning the future is not merely to raise the probability of getting and experiencing what you really want, it also involves the obligation that we have as humans. We are *custodians* of the future. It is not only immoral but obscene for us to sell out our children and the yet unborn. In a period of cataclysmic conflict between expansive trends and a finite earth, the absolute minimum that any education should dedicate itself to is *awareness of trends* and *exploration of alternatives.* No child should be the victim nor the perpetrator of violence resulting from misplanning or no planning.

Accountability requires that one be aware of alternatives, and the failure of education even to try to achieve such a goal becomes a moral crime. In the backwash of our old legal system we have not yet made such a distinction, but if the *right* to the preconditions of life is to be codified into law, denial of such rights becomes criminal. As educators we have always honored the "right to know" as an abstract principle. Now we have a basis for identifying what it is we have a right to know.

III

There are different kinds of future-creating forces, convergent and probabilistic, which need to be taught. A time predictable event, such as starvation based on population increases, is an example of the linear convergence of two variables, in this case, food and people. The cataclysmic models of *Limits to Growth* are of this type, using the interrelationship between four variables: population, pollution, resource depletion, and capital investment.

Probabilistic change is more difficult for people to understand, for it is statistical and not revealed by direct experience. The war system is probabilistic. It does not provide us with a date at which an event such as an atomic World War III will occur. Like rolling the roulette wheel, we don't know when 00 will come up. There are remote odds that it might never come up; however, we maximize our chances of prediction by assuming that there are fixed odds build into the system.

We may not win if we follow such odds, but we raise the chances of winning and reduce the chances of losing if we follow the odds. War systems are similar. By loading nuclear armament in political units (nations) capable of unilateral use of such weapons, we play nuclear roulette with the world. We can alter odds either by juggling the equipment on the world roulette wheel or by playing a new game. A new political game, removing anarchy and unilateralism from the international political game, could dramatically alter the probabilistic odds for war.

A probabilistic war system in the atomic age provides assured genocide, but we don't know when. We can, however, estimate the safety-failure probabilities and make a rough estimate of the chances of surviving each year. If we do survive another year, those who fail to understand the nature of the system begin to trust it, saying, "We haven't had atomic war so far; therefore, the system must work." But the actual probabilities for having war may continue to be the same. Like driving full speed through a city at night without lights, we had better make one of two kinds of decisions: (1) that we are apparently immune to accident, because we have not yet had one, or (2) that we are damn lucky to have gotten this far and we'd better slow down and turn on the lights. Entire national foreign policies are built on the confusion between probabilistic and convergent systems. The American "defense" system is thought by many to be an "effective deterrent" because during the period in which a weapons system called a "deterrence" system was in operation World War III did not occur. But having a "deterrence" system provides an excuse for retaining the war system, and if you don't have war while you have a war system it is in spite of the system rather than because of it.

IV

A general planning formula might include both minimal and maximal goals. For the next one hundred years the most likely threats to life are war, ecocide, and absolute poverty. *Minimal* goals are first priority goals, necessary to preserve life and provide at least the minimum conditions of social justice. But it is not enough merely to minimize threats to the continuity of life. It is necessary but not sufficient, so a decision must be to achieve minimal goals as urgently as possible, setting a specific time goal. Other time, energy, and resources should be devoted to achieving change in the direction of maximal goals. Minimal and maximal goals might be as follows:

Minimal	Maximal
Prevent cataclysmic war	Create global cooperation and world community
Prevent ecocide	Manage the world economy ecologically (stable state recycling)
Prevent absolute poverty	Create equitable sharing of resources

Clearly the goals on the right could not be reached in ten years. However, the goals on the left might be reached in ten or twenty years. Therefore tradeoffs need to be made. In the design of preferred futures, are the values on the right included as preferential values? If so, they optimize, while the values to the left are sufficient merely for survival. Should we abandon optimum goals, take half a loaf, and settle for the enormously improved but less than optimum world on the left side? Or should we use the goals on the right as preferred world goals to be achieved by the mid-Twenty-first Century, while the first state in the transition planning would target on the minimal goals on the left. Wouldn't this order our priorities and permit practical time sequences during the transition period?

The minimal values are all *survival* values. The values on the right include survival and social justice values. The next objective would seem to be the planning of environmental *quality*. This means there are three goals: (1) survival, (2) equality, and (3) quality. I would want to maximize all three, but I would have to be ready for tradeoffs when there was no other choice, and I would maximize them in the order listed.

Notice I have not listed *economic goals*. Planning involves making cost/benefit predictions, and economic costs and benefits cannot be omitted. A central dilemma of the modern world, however, is the fact that "development" has come to mean economic development. Quantitative GNP indicators have been used as indicators of "progress" through the maximization of gross economic units— whatever grotesque combination of goods and services they might produce. In market-based economic systems, *social values* are secondary to economic values, and *ecological values* come third, if at all.

In order to plan rationally there must be an estimation of economic, social, and ecological costs and benefits. And these values must also be weighed in order of priority. Since ecological values provide the life-support system, it would follow that they should be first, since they establish the perimeters and constraints under which an economic system must operate. But for what end? Surely human community and social justice are the highest goals for which we can plan. If so, social justice is more important than merely maximizing gross national products by placing economic values at top priority.

What this means is a 180-degree reversal of the priority of economic values of most Western developed nations:

Present	Future
1. Economic	1. Ecological
2. Social	2. Social
3. Ecological	3. Economic

When economics is subsumed under ecological planning, a stable state economy results. All economies must be stable state (sometimes called no-growth) eventually. The planning problem is to plan and create a post-Malthusian world rather than submit to the positive checks of starvation, pollution, resource depletion, disease, and war. "No growth" is not really a good term, for an ecologically stabilized recycling economy requires selectively planned expansion, contraction, and stabilization. The service area of the economy permits the greatest expansion while the goods economy, at least in industrialized countries, requires selective stabilization and reduction. When a stable state economy is planned on a world basis (and the sooner the better), it should be done along with a redress in the maldistribution of wealth and income. Americans, Canadians, and other overconsuming nations are likely to be threatened at first, but a new education can help affect not only the process of planning but also the transformation in personal values and lifestyle. The meaning of "standard of living" requires transformation from quantitative to qualitative criteria.

The great hazard in reduced consumption education is that it often encourages a lifestyle and an ideology based on political anarchy. But

awlessness and the anarchy of the present world that
dy of the commons." If there is to be common control
,..icluding a global peace-keeping system, unilateralism
...u individualism must operate only within the constraints of social
and ecological planning. It is clear that atomistic individualism must
give way to democratic world community if participation and
representation rather than hierarchy and coercion are to define the
world system. Not that a democratic political system can operate
without some coercion. If population expansion continues, the range
of unilateral freedom will be proportionally diminished under both a
democratic or an autocratic world system. But a participatory system
offers the greatest assurance that social justice will be realized and that
the rules we must live by are equitable.

In brief, if I were to sketch an outline of a futurist theory of
education applicable from K through graduate school, it might look
as follows:

A Futurist Educational Model

From (Current Trends)   *Toward (Preferred Future)*

1. Survival

From (Current Trends)	Toward (Preferred Future)
a. population expansion	a. population control
b. a war system	b. a peace-keeping system
c. pollution of the biosphere	c. termination of pollution
d. waste of natural resources	d. conservation recycling

2. Social Justice

From (Current Trends)	Toward (Preferred Future)
a. economic disparity	a. economic equality
b. inequality of human rights	b. equal human rights

3. Experimental Quality

From (Current Trends)	Toward (Preferred Future)
a. an ugly environment	a. a beautiful environment
b. identity given	b. identity created

This futurist theory of education is based on the following
assumptions:

1. The school cannot be neutral. It should be honest and try
to be accurate.

2. Schools help create the future by intent or by default.

3. Schools usually reinforce obsolete institutions that have become inadvertently pathological.

4. Schools should help to reconstruct the society.

5. The curriculum should be problem-centered.

6. The problems should be primarily problems of survival, social justice, and experiential quality.

7. Schools should emphasize participation in planning the future.

8. The focus should be global; spaceship earth and the human race.

9. The above broadly stated "preferred future" goals are supported by a sufficiently large informed consensus to warrant their use as social-educational goals.

10. The central task of research, inquiry, experimentation, and teaching should be to identify the means of moving from current trends toward more precisely defined preferred futures.

11. Knowledge and social action should be connected: Students should participate in social change.

12. Whenever possible, planning and social action should be based on group processes.

The model provides a feedback loop for reflection, planning, and social action. It can be psychologically sound if it begins where the student is and helps him participate in planning at his own level of experience, at first in the classroom then in the school community, then in the local community, and outward as rapidly as possible until he has a world perspective and can think of himself and behave as a member of the human race.

Much existing subject matter must be discarded or transformed: Most university and teacher education is equally vulnerable. The model challenges the claim of educational neutrality. To be neutral about the future is to perpetuate the rapidly compounding problems of the present.

On the one hand we are victims of our own experience, and so history establishes the mold of the future. Yet we are now in a period of history where we have learned enough to begin inventing the future. Each stage prepares us to apply even more creativity to historical change, thus increasing our creativity and generating new power that can provide an enormous increase to human freedom. No longer must man be a victim of the past, acting out habits over which he has no control. This new power to create new futures arrives at a fortunate time, for most of the old habits are not merely obsolete but suicidal. Clearly the mandate to education is to help facilitate this planning process, not merely for a better future, but in order to help assure that there be a future at all.

Chapter Three

Education for Survival

> *Modern institutions though sustained by knowledge*
> *also require an abundance*
> *of public ignorance to perpetuate them.*

Fear of the future increasingly corrodes modern life. We are beginning to sense the ways in which we have become locked into old institutional habits and their supporting mythologies, permitting technology and organizational technique to become the central determiners of social change. The tail usually wags the dog, and we do what is technologically possible, whether or not it is humanly desirable. Established systems become self-perpetuating and create their own goals, defining their own meaning of reality and progress. People are finally beginning to ask whether change is synonymous with progress or whether some change is destructive and even suicidal. Through our lack of qualitative standards we have often accepted all change as synonymous with social progress—the more the better. The gross national product is still the primary official indicator of national achievement. It lumps together the total dollar units of cigarette commercials and cancer therapy, automobile sales and mortuary fees, napalm and sulfa drugs.

The arrogant use of modern power has implications which are not only political and economic but ecological as well. Particularly in the West, where the Judeo-Christian traditions have flourished, man has encouraged himself to believe that he is above nature and that he can dictate to nature without showing respect for it. This arrogance is producing a dangerous ecological crisis to which the United States is the foremost contributor. The early rape and exploitation of seemingly boundless land and natural beauty still continues. The ugly consequences become more and more apparent. The beauty of irreplaceable giant redwood trees is increasingly denied to all future generations, as corporation profits and the chain saw continue to triumph over nature's ancient monuments. Lakes, streams, underground water, and even the oceans are headed rapidly toward pollution levels so high that they will be irreversible. In some areas of the United States, the air has become so polluted that it kills increasingly larger numbers of people as well as forests and vegetation. Increasingly, the birds that we don't see because of the smog are not there anyway, for our insecticides often hit wide of their mark. "Overkill" has become the symbol of our age.

Technology itself is not inherently evil, but when it develops without corresponding political, economic, and educational advances, a society becomes glutted with physical change unguided by integrated social planning. A society without control over change is a society with its future out of control. We are now at the dawn of a growing awareness that we must choose our destiny. The race is now on between more fundamental planning than we have ever engaged in and catastrophe.

Modern institutions, sustained by an immense amount of knowledge, paradoxically also require an abundance of ignorance to perpetuate them. Ignorance is the cement that continues to stabilize most contemporary institutions. Blindness to the ways in which old habits support intolerable levels of population, pollution, social inequality, and international violence is a prerequisite to the continuation of the world as it is.

Schools, also paradoxically, are usually one of the instruments for the perpetuation of ignorance. This is achieved primarily by isolating knowledge within separate compartments and by focusing on knowledge which is the least relevant, therefore meeting the traditional requirements of transmitting knowledge without disturbing the existing order. This is neither an intentional nor a stated goal of most schools, yet by isolating students from the major problems of the world the results are usually no less effective than if the goals were intended.

Schools are usually so intertwined with the larger culture (educators often proclaim that enculturation is their main objective) that they often fail to see the dangers, even the suicidal consequences, of adjusting students to obsolete aspects of the culture.

Schools that fail to develop the capacity of students to participate intelligently in the control of their society not only emasculate them but alienate them from the dominant culture. Furthermore, this approach guarantees that social decision making is kept where it is— in the hands of a few who use such power to preserve the personal advantages enjoyed only by the decision-making elite. This process, which in the past has produced social injustice, now has brought us to the point where life on this planet cannot long continue without a new relationship of both man to man and man to nature. Therefore, students are engaged in a new quest for relevance.

A Definition of Relevance

There are a variety of current uses of the world "relevance," so I would like to suggest how relevance might be defined. This will lead to a proposal for planning a relevant future through education. Then I will focus particularly on planning for survival and suggest how all this applies to social studies.

I will define an education as being relevant when it has a vital connection to human life—either to the conditions which sustain life or to the conditions which give life meaning. An education that contributes to the knowledge of health, food production, nutrition, population control, and war prevention is the kind of education which can help sustain life. Education that provides knowledge of esthetic, social, and religious quality is the kind that helps give meaning to life.

Relevance Through Planning

An education that is relevant must connect knowledge and social change so that the student becomes a causal agent in historical change. Such education should help him participate in the development of the future by directing him into the mainstream of human events, by giving him experience in making effective social decisions, and by illuminating the alternative choices and their consequences. The student should be taught to join others in cooperatively planning the future.

The essential data in all planning involves information about the direction of trends which permits likely forecasts of the future. This requires information about present conditions, historical data to plot the rate and direction of change, and projections based on locating present trends at some point in the distant future. Short-term prediction is more reliable than long-term prediction, and unexpected events may alter even short-term predictions. The purpose of planning is to minimize accidental change and to maximize intentional change. The motive for the entire enterprise is based on the unwillingness to continue what Michael Harrington has called our Accidental Century, a century which has been based on a faith in history and the marketplace and the belief that when you get into trouble you will inevitably come out smelling like roses.

Planning can occur through an elitist top-down system, or it can be based on bottom-up participation, the relative emphasis being reflective of an autocratic or democratic social philosophy. Specialists are needed in either system to provide accurate information about the consequences of alternative plans, but value judgments are necessary to define the kind of future to be planned. This role cannot be performed by a specialist. The failure of schools to help students become participants in planning processes virtually predetermines that social planning will be elitist, representing the values of those who have the power to affect social policy.

Some types of planning are already well developed, particularly in large industries. This type is well described in John Galbraith's book, *The New Industrial State*. But such planning is aimed either at anticipating trends and then adapting to them or else at manipulating the larger public into the acceptance of a goal that may serve the corporation at the expense of the larger public.

Government planning is similar, usually with even less anticipation of trends and more reliance on ad hoc crisis treatment. The manipulation of public consent is also well established, but government even includes a self-predatory addition where branches of government withhold information from other branches, each in an attempt to achieve its own special interest.

Virtually all current social planning is *expansive* planning, based on the anticipation of trends. We are told that certain kinds of jobs will be increasingly available in the next decade, with the assumption that the enterprising citizen will prepare himself to become more marketable; but another kind of planning, which might be called *reconstructive* planning, assumes that what is needed is not mainly planning *for* the future, but planning *of* the future. The reconstructive planner does not assume that people need necessarily adjust to trends but rather that trends should be adjusted to people. Reconstructive planning requires integrative social planning—with the larger social unit being given priority. If it is a question of what is good for General Motors or what is good for the American people, the latter should have the overriding claim. If it is a matter of what is good for the United States or what is good for the human race, the human race should be given priority.

The difference between expansive national defense planning and reconstructive defense planning can be illustrated as follows: The effort to build ABMs and fallout shelters to protect against the radioactivity of World War III is an example of expansive planning. The Clark-Sohn plan for World Peace Through World Law, which is designed to *avert* cataclysmic war, is an example of reconstructive planning.

Areas of Planning

In order to teach planning, it is advisable to set up areas of study. Such classifying involves the danger of once again separating problems and neglecting their interrelatedness, but some problems are more urgent than others, at least from the standpoint of survival, so distinctions in the kinds of problems permit the appropriate allocation of energy and time. Planning areas might be usefully classified under problems of (1) social justice, (2) environmental quality, and (3) survival.

Social justice involves the study of human exploitation and plans to remedy such exploitation. *Environmental quality* involves planning which increases the desirability of living in a particular society. *Survival* planning minimizes the chances of unnecessary death.

If existence does precede essence, survival planning should be given central emphasis. This is the kind of ordering understood by Martin Luther King, Jr. In spite of his deep concern for increasing social justice, he saw that it would be no victory to achieve integration of radioactive corpses. He recognized the priority of the problems of international violence in the atomic age. It is this comparative perspective that must be cultivated if planning is to order energies toward the most important problems.

Statistics are necessary but are not sufficient for describing the consequences of trends. The *meaning* of a future can be illuminated by having some sense of what it would be like to live in a world suggested by particular trends. Futurist novels, plays, any dramatic and artistic form that provides vicarious experience of alternative futures is useful to the assessment of the desirability of living in such a world. That is why novels like *1984*, films like *On the Beach* and *Seven Days in May* make future possibilities real in a way that usually cannot be achieved by statistics. It is one thing to know what the statistical probabilities are for cigarette lung cancer. But many people require a more vivid and personal event (such as the death of Edward R. Murrow) to illustrate what the statistics mean.

Planning to Survive

Four major survival problems are cataclysmic war, uncontrolled population, resource depletion, and pollution of the biosphere on which human life depends. Projections in each of these three areas give little hope that mankind can long survive. If nothing is done to change trends in any of these areas, even short-range future survival chances are very low—most of the human race is not likely to survive this century. It is increasingly possible to predict the approximate time and place where autogenocide from overpopulation, pollution, and resource depletion will take place, but the war system is somewhat different. It combines the comparatively fixed probabilities of a mutual deterrence—mutual annihilation system. Estimates of the odds for the system failing range from 1 percent to 10 percent per year. Assuming that a 2 percent per year probability of mutual annihilation is an optimistic figure, the current war system itself is not likely to get most of the human race through the twenty-first century.

The war system, however, may be one of the easier systems to reconstruct if enough people come to see that the atomic age has fundamentally transformed the meaning of national defense. Nations no longer have effective defense against nuclear arms, therefore the national "defense" they have is largely in name only. Current defense systems are examples of institutions locked into the constraints and habits of expansive planning. To move to the level of reconstructive planning requires a careful examination of alternative forms of world order. By patterning our changes according to old habits, we merely add new technology to old pre-atomic systems, giving virtually no attention to reconstructive possibilities such as an international system of national defense.

Survival and the Social Studies Teacher

The social studies programs in most schools would be transformed if they included a commitment to futurist goals directed toward the development of a world with greater social justice, improved quality of the physical environment, and increased changes for human survival. Such a commitment would provide new criteria for the selection of subject matter. History would no longer be largely an antiquarian excursion into the particular events that have come to be a dreary part of the perennial puberty rites of American youth. History should not be ignored in futurist studies, but it should be selectively studied to understand current problems. History is *always* written and studied selectively, but instead of merely chronicling battles, they could be examined not only to find out what seemed to be the primary causes but to question whether better ways might have been used to resolve the conflict. Causes of historical events include not only the precipitating factors, but also the structures that were *not* present. It is not only what people do that causes wars; it is also what they failed to do in the way of developing procedures, habits, norms, and political machinery for averting war. This use of *negative causality,* or what was omitted in the system, can be an exceedingly useful concept for analyzing historical events for the purpose of planning a future that avoids some of the pitfalls of the past.

Clearly it will be necessary to reorient our study of history to focus on those events that are the most productive. In most current history texts, very little consideration is given to the bombing of Hiroshima and the political-military implications of this nuclear era. The Nuremberg trials, the Cuban missile crisis, and the Vietnam War can be used as case studies to raise questions about the need for new principles of international law and new peace-keeping systems. The assumptions on which American policy has been based, which include atomic threat systems and a mutual deterrence theory, are crucially in need of more critical examination.

Earlier, I suggested that the four main crisis areas are war, population, resource depletion, and pollution. In all these problems, a basic strategy is to explore alternative futures and then to make comparisons of alternative goals and strategies of change as a basis for commitment to social action. New information becomes necessary. In the case of teaching about population problems, demographic and birth control information is basic. In the case of pollution, the information describing trends, danger levels, and causes becomes basic. Understanding causes should include knowledge of the resistance to pollution control offered by organizations that have a vested interest in pollution, such as the automobile industry.

But knowledge of how to bring about change must go beyond the usual mere assimilation of facts and theory. It must include direct experience. For example, if high school students were to identify a problem of air or water pollution in their own community, they could inquire into the reasons for the problem. They may find there is a lack of appropriate legislation, or lack of monitoring and enforcement. Their findings could be used to illuminate the local needs. They would at the minimum obtain more understanding of the politics of pollution control and at the maximum they would help effect actual changes. Futurist education must link theory and practice if the goal of teaching planning is to be really effective. It involves a change in the meaning of social education—away from competitive individual success, toward cooperative social action.

The basic model of reconstructive planning is not difficult to understand, but the task of reorienting a curriculum toward planning, even toward survival planning, is likely to be difficult because of the entrenched commitments to obsolete practices. The self-righteous autonomy of schools is a major obstacle. Psychologists have often defined intelligence as that which I.Q. tests measure, and the same quaint logic is often used by schools to define education as that which schools do. Without some outside theory of man, history, and the good life, schools have no outside standard of measurement and they easily commit a kind of Cartesian fallacy in which they say, "Schools are, therefore relevance exists." The most common traps include the following assumptions: (1) that state-adopted materials are necessarily relevant, (2) that the traditional content of social studies is necessarily relevant, (3) that the mass media concentrates on problems that are necessarily relevant, (4) that regents examinations and college entrance requirements are necessarily relevant, and (5) that materials prepared by university academicians are necessarily relevant. A reexamination of these assumptions may threaten the self-interest of existing bureaucracies, but may provide a breath of fresh air in the midst of the present educational stagnation.

Danger—University Ahead

The increased influence of universities on social studies curricula is a mixed blessing. To the unwary and the innocent, the university can be one more snare to trap the social studies teacher. When the university is treated as the citadel of the philosopher-king, a kind of tragic comedy can result—a case of the blind leading the blind. Theodore Roszak is even more critical:

> Until the recent rash of campus protest related to the Vietnam war, nothing has so characterized the American academic as a condition of entrenched social irrelevance, so highly developed that it would be comic if it were not sufficiently serious in its implications to stand condemned as an act of criminal delinquency. (*The Dissenting Academy*, p. 12)

"Criminal delinquency" is strong language, but a teacher who deprives his students of knowledge that might literally save his life could be said to be committing a type of criminal act. Universities often are Parkinsonian bureaucracies where words expand to fill the time available. They are often places to learn many reasons why nothing can be done—a kind of staging area for intellectual paralysis. A teacher who wants knowledge to be an instrument of action for helping people participate in social change will need to be aware that this is not the dominant meaning of knowledge in American universities. The academician carries an implicit theory of knowledge with him, and most academicians are not concerned with the kind of knowledge that makes futurist education possible.

The disciplinary compartmentalization of knowledge is one of the major traps, but even when knowledge becomes interdisciplinary, it is not necessarily relevant to the problems of our age. The new Fenton

High School Social Studies Series is a case in point. The texts are more interdisciplinary and integrative than most texts, but the particular type of inquiry method that is used is aimed at inducting students into the language and problems of behavioral *science*. The mode of inquiry is analytic and scientific. If it were also philosophical and critical, it would move beyond description into normative questions—judgments about values and questions of what ought to be, not merely what has been and what is. This would make it more suitable for futurist study. As it stands, it encourages the kind of neutrality that characterizes most behavioral science. Education for planning requires the use of scientific inquiry skills, but it also requires movement toward commitment rather than toward neutrality—an instrumental use of knowledge rather than interest in scientific inquiry as an end in itself. But Fenton himself does have social goals in mind. He points out that the students who are successful with his curriculum are not learning merely as an end in itself; the material does serve other needs—it helps them "pass the college board examinations." Middle-class "success" values once again take precedence over the more existential values of survival. What appears to be a new approach to social studies turns out not really to be an instrument of reform, but only one more way of aiming at adaptive individual middle-class success in a society that desperately needs reconstruction. The Fenton series is typical of the academic traps that reinforce old social systems under the guise of reform.

So even what is called the "new social studies" can be a way of actually preserving old ideologies. This is achieved by ignoring the more fundamental problems of our age. If by contrast we give precedence to life rather than death, beauty rather than ugliness, human equality rather than exploitation, we can then use science to see if present practices are likely to lead in such a direction. Previous illustrations have focused on social studies, but futurism is applicable to all areas of the schools. Selective use of social science, natural science, and philosophy can then become integrated educational tools that help people learn the ecological limits of human action and learn to plan the best of possible worlds.

Conclusion

This is the first period in human history where man has the means to reflect not only on his social policies, but also on the values that underlie them. His new capacity to engage in fundamental replanning, including intentional reconstruction of the culture itself, is the most important achievement of the twentieth century. This capacity is not yet being realized, yet no institute can be more useful than the schools in helping to bring this new knowledge to the general citizenry. But to do so schools must extricate themselves from many of their old habits and avoid merely trying to adapt the young to a world gone by. Schools are inextricably involved in social change, either because of what they do or what they fail to do. In an age when relevant education is desperately urgent, the ritualistic trivia and bureaucratic games that occupy most schools are not merely a waste of time but a form of pathology.

There are some old values, such as maximum freedom of choice, that are still important, but schools must *illuminate the new context* in which choices must be made. They should help students identify trends that are suicidal and also those which perpetuate social injustice and exploitation. Then the job is to collectively design optimum futures, first focusing on classes, next on schools expanding local communities, the nation, and a new world order. Such planning should include implementing and testing effective strategies for change.

If people were less alienated from the forces of social change, more aware of the problems of common survival, and more accustomed to cooperating to create the future, we could then be optimistic about the future. Schools have a crucial survival role: They can either continue to reinforce pathological trends or else by reconstructing themselves they can help divert history from the suicidal path on which it is now embarked.

Chapter Four

Reconstructive Versus Expansive Planning:
A Reconsideration of Educational Roles

> *Moving toward a world that is better—*
> *not merely bigger—*
> *requires a different education.*

Each civilization has its own gods who faithfully serve a way of life. But gods, like men, are affected by future shock. A changing world also leaves them frustrated and confused. One god, applied science, was supposed to save Western man from the ravages of nature. Not long ago good old American know-how was one of the supreme deities pouring forth a cornucopia that inundated the top and even trickled down to the bottom. Technique guided research, industry, and management. It was both a means and an end. Anyone who did not have enough wealth was confident that the Great Machine would bring him more. Then something happened. The Machine began to devour man and earth. It expanded and proliferated until it *became* the environment, until "things were in the saddle riding man."

The story is well known, yet people are so entrapped by their habits that the old system keeps churning on, like a ship without a captain. But this era of history is drawing to a close, for it is leading to self-destruction. There are three responses to the crises—one is to put on blinders, hang on tight, and ride fearlessly into oblivion; another is to understand, feel helpless, and live in profound alienation and despair; the third possibility is to help create a new era with new systems and new values. New gods must be conceived and born even before the old ones expire.

The Old Order

We live in a period of unprecedented change. New aspirations and new knowledge have led to improved sanitation, medical care, and developed industrialization. There has been a burgeoning increase in population and in goods and services. We now have more of everything: people, buildings, money, psychiatrists, aspirin, and instruments of war. Gross National Products have been the comparative measure of success among nations.

Those nations that could exploit nature most effectively could win the race for power and production. The United States has become the most effective nation for exploiting nature and producing the largest gross accumulation of things the world has ever seen. It has become the dominant model for other nations. "Development" for nearly all nations means to become similar to America, a land of businessmen and engineers.

Michael Harrington has labeled this era the "Accidental Century,"[1] a century devoid of integrated social or even economic planning. Faith in manifest destiny, the market place, and inevitable progress has encouraged the belief that when Americans get into trouble, their problems will inevitably resolve themselves.

Planning has been either individual or short-range institutional planning. The method has been ad hoc. Laissez-faire dominates the American economic system, while the word "freedom" has an aura of magic in the American value system. Americans seldom define it; its meaning is presumed to be obvious. Freedom is good, and Americans know they have it. People are "individuals"; they are all "unique" and free to take unilateral action. They are also "equal," equal to compete in the market place for an ever-large slice of an ever-larger Gross National Product. Thus the ideology of the American dream.

Reality, however, never corresponded with creed. Big corporations developed monopolies and conglomerates; and World War II wedded business to the military, though it took about fifteen years for the public to begin to be aware of the military-industrial complex. It was not until the 1960s that it began to dawn on any significant numbers of Americans that the American dream had become a nightmare. Various events revealed the nightmare—near holocaust in the Cuban missile crisis; illegality, deception, and criminal involvement in the Vietnam War; the arrogant and illegal invasions of Cuba, Laos, and Cambodia; rapid deterioration in the quality of the American environment. It is increasingly seen that habits of the past that had once held a measure of adaptability were turning into formulas for suicide. America, the hope of the future, had entered the atomic age and the ecological age with a preatomic military outlook and an engineering mentality. War in the atomic age has become obsolete and national defense has become impossible, but the Pentagon keeps rolling along. The engineering approach to the exploitation of nature has become impossible; but the engineering outlook still dominates, and corporation presidents cry about the environment all the way to the bank.

Much of American culture has become obsolete. Even worse, it has become a threat to the continuation of human life. It is more exploitative than adaptive. It does not base its principles on either social or biological ecology. It is acquisitive and predatory. In a fundamental metaphysical sense it is an instrument for alienation—of man from man and man from nature. Unfortunately, most other modern industrial nations share many of the same characteristics and common aspirations.

Youths, who are less rooted in the preatomic and pre-ecological world, find it easier to understand some of the elements of cultural pathology. They hear the protests of minorities and have discovered the plight of millions of Americans who are not even receiving justice according to the old rules. Resentment, cynicism, and despair have led many of the young to withdraw into youth enclaves, seeking some form of direct community within a society they consider "sick." Others, through love, lead protests for the reform and renewal of America; still others, through hate, want to burn and destroy.

True believers in the old values have tried to lump together all forms of youthful defiance and to dismiss the youth movement as communist-led, but it has become obvious that many young people are not even interested in structural reform, let alone revolution. Many want only freedom to practice new personal lifestyles.

As a result of the Vietnam War, it has become increasingly difficult even for those who are rooted in the old values to avoid questioning public policy. The myth that supported pax Americana, to save the free world from the devil of communism, began to disintegrate. "Free world" leaders in South Vietnam and elsewhere were too often among the most despotic, corrupt, and antidemocratic forces in the world.

By the early 1970s, a new American consensus was being built around the unpopularity of the Vietnam War. But an even more crucial consensus is being built on common agreement that the environment is becoming unlivable. Neither the rich nor the poor, the young nor the old, the white nor the black can breathe polluted air or drink polluted water without bad effects. The ecology movement is not merely one more ideology, unless survival itself could be called an ideology. In Russia, Lake Bakal and the Volga River are going the way of Lake Erie and the Mississippi. The biosphere is becoming more fundamental than the ideologies of either Adam Smith or Karl Marx.

Most schools have been instruments for the reinforcement of the old era of quantitative expansion. They have been symbiotic partners contributing to an even larger economy, keeping the old culture intact by ignoring the domestic and international crisis and the injustices in which the United States has been deeply involved. The post-Sputnik, federally-sponsored science programs, and the generally willing disposition of American teachers and researchers to tailor curricula and research according to the formulas for acquiring funds, have produced a military-industrial-educational complex which continues to have a vested interest in the old order.

The schools have provided two ingredients for reinforcing the old order: (1) *knowledge* of the kind that contributes to technique and efficiency in an industrial society, including science, literacy, a work ethic, competitive success values, and organizational skills; and (2) *absence* of experience in social planning and social change. Students have been processed by the schools for success within the old system, but they have been equally processed for impotence within the new order. To be sure, there are a few teachers who are not teaching for the old order; and so there are youths who have not been miseducated and who are ready to form the leadership for a new kind of education. Yet most schools have often been so ineffective that they have often failed to achieve even their obsolete goals.

In short, when schools are instruments of *expansive* planning, they merely serve the objectives of the old order. That is why educational theory must now distinguish sharply between two forms of planning. These two forms might be identified by labels such as linear versus ecological or quantitative versus qualitative. For the purpose of this chapter, however, I shall call them expansive versus reconstructive.

The New Order

Expansive planning, as I have noted, is already deeply ingrained in the old order. The expansive process started long before World War II, and planning for expansionary goals continued as an intentional objective, following the warfare state of World War II. Increasingly, industry and government (especially through military spending) applied rational techniques to the planning of production systems. The consolidation and expansion of political power within both government and industry often became a primary, *unofficial* objective. But the expansive planning formula was the *official* policy for guiding change. Logical analysis and empirical data were applied to an economic cost/benefit formula. The objective was to predict and control variables to maximize economic profit. Costs would be justified if they contributed to higher benefits. Econometric techniques were developed and taught in universities, and the gap between prediction and results diminished. Economics became a new "science." The Edsel was launched in the 1950s without rigorous cost/benefit studies. But Mustang merchants of the 1960s did their homework.

Cost/benefit analysis under expansive planning has been concerned with *economic* benefit. It is a "how to make money with less risk" process. *Reconstructive planning would include economic cost/ benefit criteria, but it would subsume economic objectives under two higher priorities: (1) ecological planning and (2) social planning.* The rationale is that ecological goals are needed to preserve the biosphere, and the biological prerequisites for life supercede all other categories. Given a world where life is still possible, the next objective is to put man instead of technology at the center of the scene to maximize the quality of life in the social order. The old order lets the technological tail wag the social dog.

New Norms

Any form of planning increases predictability. Current expansive planning increasingly permits us to tell young people that they should prepare for certain types of jobs because these will constitute the manpower needs of the near future. The enterprising citizen in such a system should prepare himself to be more marketable. Then he is a "good" citizen and he is likely to become "successful." Our educational system, in both the classroom and the counseling office, has been reinforcing this planning model.

All planning requires base-line information about trends, which means sufficient data to plot the rate and direction of change. But expansive planning assumes that people must adapt to the direction of change. It does not assume that the direction of change might be wrong and that the forces of social change should be more fundamentally controlled by the people affected by the change. Therefore, population expansion, technological development, and profit making create change to which people should adapt.

Reconstructive planning, on the other hand, carries us to a new social stage. It requires a new education to initiate it and it reeducates those who become involved in it. It assumes that what is needed is not mainly planning *for* the future, but planning *of* the future. It assumes that trends should be adjusted to people rather than people to trends. It requires anticipation not only of trends, but *illumination of the varieties of possible futures* so that people can plan to have the kind of society they really want. It requires a shift to macrocosmic science from microcosmic science. Knowledge that is organized into compartmentalized subject areas has little use in reconstructive planning.

Reconstructive planning also moves beyond band-aid ad hoc treatment of social problems to consider the possible need for larger-scale reform. It tries to look at the *total* system, not primarily for increasing technical efficiency, but for survival and for improving the quality of life.

Reconstructive planning will not only require information specialists, but it will require professional planners who can use the results of participatory processes to identify those goals people consider desirable and to establish a framework of ecologically possible futures.

For instance, our "national defense" system is an example of expansive planning. It includes expanding not only nuclear capacity, but also distribution and sales of military hardware to smaller countries. If present trends continue, $4 trillion will be spent globally in the 1970s in the name of national defense. Expanding national military systems will recruit and conscript millions of young men. Smaller nations will move toward overkill capacity while "advanced" nations escalate overkill.

Reconstructive planning would not expand the war-making capacity of present systems but would move toward the development of a global system of conflict management. The goal would be to avert cataclysmic war. Therefore the means would not include increasing the technology of cataclysm by expanding present systems. Rather it would reconstruct present political and legal systems so that an effective international peace-keeping system can operate. Military funds could be transferred to social environmental needs. International politics would move from anarchy and competition to community and cooperation.

Education as Social Experience

Neither a laissez-faire society nor one based on expansive planning has any basis for identifying relevant social goals. In a laissez-faire system the goals are individual. In an expansive system the goals are corporate, quantitative, and technical—the power to achieve goals becomes a goal in and of itself.

Reconstructive planning assumes that the *processes* in which people become involved constitute their education. Education cannot be assigned to designated "schools" while economic, military, and political institutions are treated as separate, non-educational units of the society. Under a reconstructive model, people are not mere instruments that add to the efficiency of the social machine. People become what they do; they are transformed by roles and experiences of the society in which they live. This is the way unplanned cultures acquire their persistent conservatism.

If a culture is suicidal, as our pre-atomic culture now is, it requires extraordinary insight, new theory, and great initiative to make an intentional qualitative transformation of the culture. To understand the old culture is to begin that transformation—for the perpetuation of a culture is based on its being *believed;* the transformation is based on its being *understood.*

To understand one's culture, it is useful to have experience in other ways of living, in other value systems. Cross-cultural and cross-valuational experiences can result from living in other countries, with different social classes, or by means of art and literature that communicate other ways of living.

We need to understand where our own society is going if we are to see the need for alternatives. This requires predictive information based on current trends. But it also requires illumination of other possible futures as well as an education that helps us to design the future and to engage in educational and political action that will help bring it into being. Not only schools but all other institutions need to be used to produce the necessary change. Accordingly, schools as we have known them will be less needed. For education will result from living in a reconstructed social order since the social order will have humanizing goals that are synonymous with education in its most basic sense.

Man in Nature Versus Man over Nature

The reconstruction of a culture requires transformation of the premises on which it is based. Each culture has its own conception of nature. The Judaeo-Christian emphasis upon man's dominion over nature has provided a metaphysic to support an arrogant and suicidal exploitation of nature. Whereas many other cultures begin with the assumption that man is part of nature and should seek harmony with nature, Western man's belief that he stands above nature has encouraged him to rape and exploit it. What is now needed is a reconstruction of man's relations to nature. A revolution in Western theology away from the man-nature dualism toward an ecological way of life is now required. Lake Erie is nearly dead, forests are dying from smog, birds of dying of pollution, and man is part of the life chain. Man will either be forced into a new relationship with nature or will perish from his ignorance.

The United States, the "number-one" nation in Gross National Product, is also the "number-one" nation in gross pollution and exploitation of nature. Expansive planning takes little or no account of ecological responsibility. When executives plan for developing and marketing automobiles, they give primary consideration to corporate profits rather than to whether the internal combustion engine should be used in the automobile. Nor do they dedicate themselves to larger questions of transportation—whether, for example, the automobile should continue as the dominant form of public transportation. Without a system of reconstructive planning, we fail to make the necessary public decisions, thus guaranteeing the continued tyranny of the automobile. Without new forms of planning the old forms may continue by default. By centering on economic expression man will continue to exploit and destroy nature and therefore himself.

The Quest for Relevance

The word "relevance" is used by those who want to change the existing social order. It implies that the present society lacks meaning. In general, we might say that a society and the educational experiences it provides are "relevant" when they generate a vital connection either with the conditions which sustain life or with the conditions that give life meaning. Modern America, increasingly, is a cultural system that threatens life more than it sustains life. For it deprives people of meaning, substituting a predatory culture for one that is life affirming and coherent.

A culture that substitutes expansive planning and profit making for environmental quality and social justice is not only one that persists in being irrelevant to many current human needs but one that provokes a growing despair about the future. A society that is so locked into its old habits that it cannot even take human survival seriously is desperately irrelevant.

Once man understands that he can only do what nature permits he will be forced to take account of ecology, the relationships between organisms and their environment. Ecological systems are independent, recycling, life-supporting systems. Each living creature has a niche within an ecological subsystem, and every such subsystem is part of a global macrosystem. Global ecology is therefore an ultimate determiner of life on planet Earth.

When man changes his environment, he affects the global ecological system. When he acts merely as an engineer, contributing to expansive planning, he acts with ecological blinders, changing the ecosystem in unanticipated ways. When physical engineering principles are given priority over biological systems, the stage is set for disaster.

The shift to ecological criteria will require reconstruction of dominant trends in modern thought. The concepts of "progress," "modernization," and "standards of living," which underlie life in the "advanced" countries, must undergo revolutionary transformation if human life is to continue.

The basic conflict is between the closed system and the open system. The thrust of modern thought is process-oriented and open. Change is subject to no constraint. The frontier metaphor still dominates, for the world is thought to be an unlimited horizon, forever up for grabs. Ecological planning does not preclude change, but it requires first knowing enough to know what it is that we do not know in order to subdue engineering arrogance. Moreover, it requires that research be conducted as rapidly as possible toward understanding enough about ecosystems to make a rational ecological cost/benefit estimate as to whether each risk is really worth the price.

One of the main constraints upon planning is energy. Most of the present economic development uses stored fossil fuels, which are being rapidly depleted. Incoming energy from the sun and the tides could be expanded; but when fossil fuels are exhausted, usable incoming energy will probably provide only a fraction of the replacement at current use levels. So nuclear energy is considered the panacea by expansive planners.

Nuclear fission, however, produces dangerous, prolonged by-products for which no adequate disposal has been found. Reactors are capable of producing enormous radioactivity if accidents occur, and some accidents do occur. Fusion energy is a different matter. If it can be developed, it will be relatively safe and abundant. *But by no means is it certain that practical methods of controlling fusion energy will be found.* Expansive planning, relying on technological breakthroughs, assumes that "it must be found, therefore it will be found." If this technofanatic faith does not pay off, modern civilization that is locked in to an expansive formula will become a disaster when energy sources are depleted and reduced rather than expanded.

It is estimated that if all people on Earth used energy at the American level, fossil fuels would be exhausted in eighteen months. The usual projections of a few more decades on oil reserves, or a century or more on coal, are based on present rates of consumption in which the poor of the world use only about one fiftieth the energy of the affluent on a per capita basis. If fusion or other free energy sources do not materialize, the American standard of living cannot long continue. In the meantime, under the present system, the industrialized countries exhaust irreplaceable resources in an orgy of waste while most of the world lives in poverty. Those with power over resources also exert veto power over all future generations. A sane thermodynamic policy would require a global system of resource allocation with policies based on current ecological criteria. Then, if fusion energy does become available, it will be as a bonus. A sane energy policy could not be based on present high risks of expansive planning which lock development into a course that requires exponentially increasing energy sources.

Life in a stabilized energy system would require conversion of quantitative growth economics into a no-growth or initially into a minus-growth system; and it would require that lifestyles in overdeveloped nations be drastically altered so that the economy would be sustained on the basis of incoming energy. The expansive frontier would be over, but the experiential *quality* frontier would be at a take-off point. Knowledge and experience can now be the new resource, and mankind can enter a new age in which meaning rather than accumulation becomes primary.

If the American people can begin to make headway toward reconstructive planning, they may find that the central areas of concern include (1) survival, (2) social justice, and (3) environmental quality. Planning directed toward *survival* minimizes chances of unnecessary death; toward *social justice* minimizes human exploitation; and toward *environmental quality* increases the desirability of our social-physical environment.

The current quest for relevance is itself an indication of the ever-growing desire to order social priorities. Reconstructive planning requires that people attempt to agree on the kind of future they really want, which involves ordering priorities. Martin Luther King, Jr. not only understood the need for social justice; but he also saw that unless international violence could be controlled, there would be little victory in the integration of radioactive corpses. If "existence does precede essence,"[2] a perspective must be developed which will give primary emphasis to survival goals and to the allocation of time and energy to achieve them.

In an age when preatomic war systems threaten the existence of the human race, antiwar planning should be given a top priority. But neither in the earlier laissez-faire system nor in the current expansive planning system is there a basis for this kind of historical-global comparative perspective. Expansive systems keep men locked into old goals. Established institutions become king, and people become pawns. Compare the relative effort the United States puts into the expansion and development of the present war system versus the effort put into disarmament negotiation and international peace-keeping plans.

The Transition: Breaking the Mold

To break the constrictions of pathological habits, it is necessary to reorganize the gulf between the kind of world we might have and the world that is. The possible world of the future should not be described, as it usually is, merely by technologists. It must also be described by artists, by conservationists, and by people exploited within the present society. The rich, the poor, and the "silent majorities"—all should begin to dream of the kind of life they really wish to have through an open dialogue of proposals, models, visions. Citizens then become artists rather than merely manpower. As ecologically possible goals are clarified, attention can be given to social priorities.

Social assessments rather than GNP should become the central indicators of national progress. Such assessments need to compare the social consequences of $80 billion a year spent by the United States for instruments of war and annihilation versus the consequences if such funds were spent to alleviate hunger, sickness, and ignorance.

The idea industries—schools, universities, research and development industries, and the media—each performs crucial roles in shifting to a reconstructive society. Although currently they contribute primarily to the expansive systems of the old order, there is some indication of growing awareness that our problems are problems of human survival. Even the affluent live in a world engulfed by crime, congestion, pollution, ugliness, and war. Fundamental reform offers some advantages for everyone.

Criticism is a distinguishing feature of any intellectually open society, but the mass media have been as derelict as the schools in accepting the obligation for basic criticism. One salutary effect of the Johnson administration in the area of foreign policy was to begin to force schools and mass media more into the role of independent critics instead of faithful loyalists. When the theatre of the absurd gave regular performances on Capitol Hill, the traditional royalist role became increasingly impossible.

It is now imperative to extend the same spirit of criticism that has been directed primarily toward the Vietnam War into all areas of American society. Without discriminating between the sense and the nonsense that constitutes their heritage, Americans are overcome by the flood of history, so that they lack a basis for diverting the flow. Only if mass media and the schools can provide basic criticism can they be transformed into instruments of liberation instead of instruments of suppression. Then the cycle of ignorance, so essential to the maintenance of the old way of life, may be broken.

But new visions are not sufficient. We need also to increase the people's power to change institutions. The draft, military interventionism, and civil rights issues all have helped politicize a society that previously slumbered in political apathy. Under the old order people had been taught not to be political. Those who appealed to their constitutional rights have often been branded as un-American and had their jobs threatened and often eliminated.

Political action should be not only a right, but an obligation. Anything less implies that normal behavior does not involve participation in the control of change. A non-participatory society is not a democratic society. In most of American society—industry and the military are prime examples—roles are allocated by an elite. Participation in the change of the institution is tightly regulated. Yet participation in change not only integrates a society, though not without conflict; it breaks down the rigid structures of institutions. It forces institutions to serve people, and it constitutes a basic strategy for democratic change rather than encouraging the revolutionary violence that may become necessary when institutional rigidity persists too long.

The American military constitutes a prime example of non-reconstructive education. Instead of participation, obedience is taught. Instead of criticizing and choosing between value systems, ideological indoctrination is used. The soldier is identified as manpower, a cog in the military machine. The kind of education provided by military experience is in opposition to the kind of reconstructive education that is needed. The military is one of the best examples of a negative educational model—one that dehumanizes and is committed to expansive planning and technology for war-making purposes. In searching for an idea of education for survival, it is useful to develop a model of education for annihilation. The Army Corps of Engineers is equally an excellent negative model for ecological planning, well deserving of its title of public enemy number one among conservationists.

The record of public irresponsibility is so great on the part of many profit-making businesses that it encourages people to recommend economic systems that allow for no profit making at all. But some profit-making areas may not be predatory, and a participatory or reconstructive society would have to work out experimentally a new balance between private profit and public interest, making sure that profit making does not continue to control social change. What is clear in American society is that business activities must be far more circumscribed by public control. The use of natural resources should not be determined by profit in the market place. Many resources are scarce and irreplaceable, requiring public control.

Commerce should not determine where it is necessary for people to live. Rather commerce should move to where people desire to live. People have always been forced to live where jobs are available. This is currently a major reason for the problems of the burgeoning metropolis. Entire cities need to be planned anew, taking into account the ecology and the human conditions necessary for a good society. Economic goals have determined where our cities are now located. Business should therefore follow, not determine, social objectives that take into account the combined aesthetic, religious, social, economic, and ecological needs of the people.

Transformation of the present economic system will be no easy matter. For ideologies supportive of the old order are taught within and transmitted through the immense power of profit-making businesses. When businessmen say that they are only giving people what they want, they themselves often fail to admit or to understand that the business system has taught them what to want and has severely restricted other alternatives.

To unlock present businesses from the military-industrial complex will also be difficult. Profit making and war making have become fused into a way of life. People idolize whatever gives them livelihood; so when a nation gives so much of its wealth to make instruments of death, it is necessary to create an ideology to justify that way of life.

Replanning must therefore be realistic about ideological obstacles to be overcome. One obstacle is the myth that a war system produces prosperity. It temporarily stimulates the economy and provides immense profits to a few; but it fails to provide the more useful long-run forms of investment capital, and it wastes the resources and energies of a nation in antisocial activity. The result is a decline in growth even of the quantitative GNP along with inflated prices for consumer goods.

One irony of American life is that the official ideology describes a largely free enterprise economy, while in fact both business and government have created a form of socialism for the rich. Businesses are often ready to sacrifice the old ideology when it is profitable to do so, but public policy has made it more profitable to support war systems than peace systems. If labor and industry are to disconnect themselves from a war system, there will have to be equally attractive plans for finding livelihood in other ways. This means that transition plans for peace should provide economic security by transferring military funds into a peace economy. So far this has been obvious in principle but lacking in political support, for there is no political alliance devoted to peace which is as strong as the military-industrial alliance.

Labor and industry are not likely to be a political hindrance to reconstructive planning if they can be economically rewarded, but there is little chance of extricating the American economy from the old war system if the people fear the prospect of unemployment. The reduction in contracts for the aerospace industries under the Nixon administration may have given the appearance that the war system is being dismantled. But widespread unemployment resulting from failure to convert to peace planning produces reactionary fear and invites further establishment of the old system. People will not accept unemployment, though they will accept systems change from war to peace if peace guarantees economic security. This would require a new political economy which is not limited to socialism for the rich.

From Tinkering to Systems Change
The one habit that most frequently locks Americans into expansive planning is reliance on reform of existing systems by voluntary, unilateral action. For example, when a business is asked to stop polluting, the businessman calculates the costs of such action and his profit margin compared with other industries that pollute. He may be in a tight squeeze with respect to profits; and even if he does not want

to be a polluter, he may not be willing to change his industry if the other industries continue polluting.

However, if there is a multilateral decision, so that all businesses uniformly agree or are uniformly required to stop pollution, a systems change can result. Traditionally Americans have considered the use of federal controls to be restrictions on their "freedom." Yet, when the question of federal control was raised in a poll of American captains of industry (in a 1970 *Fortune* survey[3]) most of the elite of business leadership *wanted* the federal government to step in, set standards, and regulate activities related to environment.

Pollution would not be stopped if the only choice were to have these corporate executives stop pollution on their own volition. Some critics would therefore consider business executives to be evil and antisocial. Yet, the central problem is that *in a market system* their unwillingness to cooperate makes sense because economic self-interest is primary. In a market system, social improvement must either be accidental or compatible with profit. When pollution control moves out of the market system and into a public system, it makes sense for everyone. The costs are passed on uniformly and no single industry finds itself at a competitive disadvantage. Social and environmental values take priority, leaving the market to operate within necessary constraints.

When the same analysis is applied to war systems, we can see that the Pentagon's desire to expand and improve weapons systems is not the result of a subhuman species who inhabit the Pentagon. It is a sensible decision within the framework of the old nation-state military threat system. In such a preatomic context the question is whether to have good national defense or a poor one. The answer is obvious. Whether to have a nation-state system of defense or a multilateral global system is an entirely different question. With new systems as alternatives, the options expand considerably. We can then examine whether it is really possible to make preatomic systems work in the atomic era or whether new political arrangements are necessary. *We don't look for the new answers unless we ask the new questions.*

In much of our society we can pose parallel alternatives: is a charity system for the poor a way of solving or of perpetuating poverty? Are there more effective systems for redistributing wealth?

Should the alienation of people be treated mainly on an individual therapeutic basis, or is alienation mainly a function of social, economic, and political structure? If so, what structural changes are necessary? Should medical care be mainly an individual problem to be ironed out between each citizen and his doctor, or should both quality and access be an obligation of the larger society, guaranteed by law? All of these options pose problems in their conventional expansive context and then suggest alternative solutions within a systems change. The entire range of questions and alternatives can be posed not only within the framework of a nation but within the world biosphere and the entire international arena. Pollution, war, poverty, alienation, medical care, and other human problems can be approached more adequately than they have been if there are systems changes within nations. But the international system might not change, and therefore unilateral relationships between nations would continue on the international level. The human race would be unrepresented. A global human and ecological perspective is necessary for the solution of major problems. Anything less will solve some and only compound others, often causing regression in the name of progress.

Planning New Systems

When planning includes economic and political systems change, an entirely new future becomes possible. How can we make sense out of the apparent belief of some people that they want an end to war and to poverty when we see their remarkable failure to move toward those ends? Currently virtually all planning consists of subsystem planning, where our formal and informal education teaches us to perceive of change only *within* existing systems.

Let us assume that we are emerging from the cocoon of the old order. We shift from individual economic objectives into moral and survival objectives. We say, "No more war! No more poverty!" Even without further research, enough existing knowledge is probably available to achieve both of these goals. We fail to move toward such goals because few people consider them viable goals. They do not seem viable because they require systems change; and people have been living, psychologically, in another system. The system they live in reinforces those assumptions that are required to perpetuate the system. The prophecy of war and poverty becomes self-fulfilled. Are we all so encased in such traps that we will inevitably join the lemming, and do it brilliantly with the aid of computers?

Determinism Versus Human Potentiality

If human learning resulted merely from conditioning and reinforcement, there would be little basis for optimism. "Systems lock-in" would probably be altered only by World War III or widespread ecocide. The only hope seems to be in understanding processes rather than being victimized by them. This is within the framework of human potentiality, but it is not within the framework of the experience of more than a fraction of the people on this planet. Most people have been conditioned to roles, and they treat conventions as ultimate religion.

But this in itself provides a major clue for the kind of education that is needed. It must not train people in skills without also helping them to understand and to be critical of the uses for which these skills can be applied. It is one thing to learn to write; it is quite another willingly to use good English to deceive.

A new education requires as a major prerequisite that we be "on top" of the games we play, whether they be mathematical, economic, or legal. It would permit us to use images and symbols rather than to be victimized by them. The capacity of man to invent his own symbolic games permits him to invent and therefore reconstruct his own culture. Some of this intentional value design has already started, but it is a stage of consciousness that has only been possible in our own period of human history, where the social sciences have provided some understanding of interconnections between thought, culture, and personality. Culture has always changed, usually slowly and unintentionally, held tightly in constraint by supposedly sacred assumptions about man and the universe. Now, however, culture can be changed *intentionally*. This capacity may prove to be the most significant achievement in the history of man. It permits him to invent and therefore to design values, society, and history. But if he is to have this new freedom he must exchange it for the old.

Teaching Reconstructive Planning through the Schools

Schools have reinforced the old order mainly by failing to illuminate alternatives. Universities have been directly a part of the expansive system working on war research, training military officers in ROTC programs, and training management in the theory of expansive planning. They have also contributed to the old order by preparing technically trained manpower for the job market. The "liberal arts" have often been devoted to leisure or status activities rather than to humanistic planning. Elementary schools and high school have been largely dominated by the colleges and the universities. Teachers are products of higher education; most materials they use are developed by professors in ideological cooperation with publishing industries in which the old order has usually been perpetuated.

A basic problem is the lack of relevance of schools to the dominant issues of our age. When knowledge is organized in such a manner as to hinder people from having control over the power structure that supports their social order, the result is to reinforce the status quo. The phrase "knowledge explosion" usually refers to the kind of knowledge that serves expansive planning. Most of this knowledge is atomistic, technical, and designed for existing institutional structures. Teaching machines and the "new" math, science, and social science have focused on knowledge which often has minimum relevance to the central human problems of our age. Instead it has focused on knowledge related to the problems of academic disciplines. Virtually none of the exploding knowledge treats alternatives strategies for war prevention, while much of it provides the mathematical and scientific know-how to expand the efficiency of current war systems.

Education for survival clearly requires a reversal of these trends, in which reconstructive planning is at the center rather than the periphery of the curriculum. Knowledge should be mainly organic, holistic, integrative, and ecological. The focus should be on identifying central problems of the future as they are developing in the present and on gaining knowledge that permits people to control institutions and technology so that they serve the real interests of people.

The old order consists not only of what we have done but also of how we have done it. The way in which we have come to think and live has been reinforced by the schools. We put life into compartments, for specialization has increased industrial efficiency. Knowledge is compartmentalized (by subjects), thought and emotion are separated (by "objectivity"), and theory and practice are separated (learn now, do later). Experience is cut up into time slots (courses) so that real problems must be avoided, since it is not possible to specify the exact time for social projects to come to fruition. By atomizing the human personality we make it impossible for schools to integrate the society.

Education for reconstructive planning requires integration of thought and emotion, and theory and practice; it requires widening social experience. It does not preclude specialization, but it does preclude merely specializing. We should no longer develop a trained cripple to fit into a dehumanized society, but we continue to do so in virtually all schools. the person who is to participate in the development of a humane society must be helped to become a whole person in relation to nature and society.

Fortunately, young people are increasingly able to develop their own culture and escape from the miseducation of the old order. But merely to escape from the old order often produces politically ineffective subgroups, who produce new variations on the old theme of individualism without effectively changing the system. The old order can be reinforced either directly or by default. To change existing structures requires a new theory of education and of politics and an integration of the two.

Neutrality and Objectivity

One of our major educational myths is the belief in "objectivity." The scholar is said to be morally neutral and concerned only with truth. This view is itself part of the ideology of the old order, for it excuses the scholar and researcher from having a theory of social relevance. It also permits him to be accountable only to scientific standards of research methodology and the judgment of his peers, who are usually success products of the same system.

The knowledge used in reconstructive planning should be scientific and accurate. The highest standards of intellectual honesty and the best methods of obtaining accurate information must be used. The new focus of inquiry, however, must be shifted to a different set of questions; and knowledge must be aimed at functional social integration rather than neutral atomism. The intellectual process is part of the social order, and it can share in reconstructing that order only by reconstructing itself.

For example, between 1968 and 1970 at the University of Hawaii a small group of students and faculty began to focus on futurism and planning. Central attention was given to the kind of Hawaii that was possible by the year 2000, and the kind of Hawaii that was developing. What had been developing was air, water, and noise pollution. An obsolete transportation system and uncontrolled expansion had reduced the aesthetic and social quality of life. It had glutted the roads with traffic and created some of the world's highest housing costs. These problems were illuminated by faculty planners and students, and the local papers not only gave coverage to planning proposals but were highly supportive of the new interests in futurism.

These pressures generated political repercussions. More attention was given by the governor and the legislature to planning questions. By early 1971, there was evidence that planning would be a central political issue of the next election; and, though the problems of reconstructive planning were only beginning to be considered, the University was starting to consider itself as an instrument of social planning. Many problems were seen to be unsolvable without basic reconstructive planning.

Planning for the state government and for the schools had been based on projections of population trends. A group of students and faculty proposed a plan for population control and dispersal throughout the state. It was first dismissed as absurd by politicians; but during 1971, controlled population dispersal was studied and even advocated by the governor and his staff—a shift from an expansive to a reconstructive outlook.

A small number of the students and faculty of the university were beginning to effect the planning theory of the state, not by being "neutral" but by being responsible, relevant, and involved. The old neutrality had been one of the reasons for the problems they confronted.

When planning frames of reference expand beyond the local area, as they must, then problems of war, population, pollution of the planetary biosphere, and sharing of the resources of the earth become interrelated. Needed political and legal reforms become planning problems; therefore they become educational problems. Research is transformed accordingly. Ecological mapping and the use of social indicators provide basic research data, preceding the process of policy analysis and design.

Cultural Reconstruction

Reconstructive planning involves cultural reconstruction. It involves change in the power structure, social structure, and ideology of a nation. Most American schools are themselves so much a part of the culture that they selectively omit the kind of study that provides critical awareness of the way in which the society is ordered, the way in which values are usually shaped, and the specific values that constitute the American way of life. Americans tend to universalize the beliefs that they have been taught, since they have no way of distinguishing between human nature in any universal meaning and the particular values of their own culture.

They often proclaim that man is naturally aggressive, naturally competitive, and naturally motivated by self-interest. To these assumptions about human nature are added other myths about innate intelligence and educability. Natural rights of individuals and "laws" of supply and demand are assumed to be part of nature.

These notions are often treated as absolute, metaphysical laws to be held with self-righteous certainty. Such piety inhibits the reconstruction of the culture and encourages a self-righteous foreign policy that is more concerned with the techniques of implementation than with justification of its goals. Other ways of life are perceived as inferior. Other political and economic forms are seen as "wrong," and foreign policy becomes a holy war. Students from our "leading" universities have generally found it easy to serve government or industry and to fit into prevailing lifestyles and conventional ideologies because their schools have seldom served the very process of criticism that might make them contributors to an open democratic society. They usually serve the objective of understanding democratic political *forms* without creating political or cultural awareness and without opening up a radical range of value alternatives. Democratic values are applied to social and political theory but are often omitted from economics, where democratic control is taboo. The student is supposed to feel "free" (to get a job) when he has his diploma and certification, though he is still locked into the ubiquitous value system of his culture.

It would be an exaggeration to claim that virtually no student escapes. Increasingly some do escape, even forming various kinds of countercultures—radical reformist and alienated escapist. But countercultures too often consist of absolutistic negations of conventional values. The real educational revolution would occur if schools begin to maximize awareness of current cultural values and alternative possibilities. Schools can do this in a number of ways. One is to shift from middle-class American values to cross-cultural comparisons. Non-Western cultures offer a vivid contrast, but direct experience and study of the various ethnic varieties within the Western world itself can be helpful. Experiencing differences between lower and middle-class lifestyles in the local "community" (as we erroneously call it) should be a normal part of American education. The role of political, economic, and social ideologies is conspicuously neglected in most schools. Economics is often taught as a value-neutral science, even though the actual use of economics must always be within a cultural-political-ideological context. The typical alliance between university departments of economics and schools of business is not coincidental.

Most American elementary schools substitute the state for the church and directly indoctrinate nationalism. In high school, and even more so in colleges and universities, indoctrination is sometimes less direct. It occurs primarily through omission of cultural criticism; the content of academic subjects is studied rather than the cultural content and the problems of society. The war system has a pervasive effect on all of American life, and yet nationalistic assumptions, human nature myths, and the economic complex that supports and embraces its ideology are rarely the subject of inquiry in most American education. If half as much time were spent studying the assumptions on which American militarism is based as is spent on indoctrinating young men into military systems through Junior and Senior ROTC, the curricula of American schools would be substantially modified. Schools should be analyzing the assumptions of a deterrence policy and designing peace-keeping systems instead of perpetuating war systems.

Moreover, the great disparity in the distribution of wealth within the United States and between countries is supported by very questionable, but seldom questioned, ideologies. The schools should help students examine the ways in which ideology and culture are related to power and privilege. Even those who are exploited usually accept the ideologies which support their exploitation. Until Americans have a basis for questioning the assumptions upon which their own maldistribution of wealth is based they are hardly in a position to serve as anything except an obstacle in reconstructing economic systems throughout the world. This means examining and redesigning the political rules that permit some Americans (the billionaires) to receive about $50,000 *an hour,* while millions of people in the same nation receive $5 *an hour* because it is the minimum prescribed by law. Over half of the world's people receive less than *50 cents a day.* Gaps in income ratios of ten to one are sometimes sufficient to cause reevaluation. In a world where the gap between the rich and the poor nations is widening, and where it is not closing even between the rich and poor in the United States, there is a central moral obligation of schools to help students redesign the economic game plan. Students will soon discover, if they have not already, that "monopoly" is not merely a parlor game (1980s figures above).

The next step is to design a just economic system in order to convert an economics-centered culture into a society-centered culture. Transition strategies should take account of the way in which inequality produces tension, conflict, and violence plus the enormous amount of police and military coercion that is required to perpetuate economic injustice. Absolute poverty kills biologically, while relative poverty destroys psychologically; and both produce social disintegration and low levels of creativity.

But transition from the old to the new order also requires analysis of the many devices that produce inequality. Redistribution rules would require new income taxes, new corporation taxes, price controls, wage controls, and educational equality. Current taxes such as long-term capital gain, mineral depletion allowances, tax-free municipal bonds, and the many tax devices that provide preferential treatment for the wealthy need to be understood in relation to the creation of poverty and the ideology of expansive planning. Then a means-end plan for restructuring economic systems at both a national and global level can be developed.

Participation in Change

Reconstructive planning requires knowledge of alternative systems, experience in designing the future, and direct participation in creating change. Ralph Nader's raiders provide an excellent model of participative education. Law students voluntarily joined him in investigating ways in which industry and government exploit the public. When an investigator has the evidence to expose a department or industry, he becomes directly involved in political action by lobbying and by use of mass media. None of this is outside the legitimate functions of educational institutions. Students should be encouraged to give careful attention to the design of the future so that it serves the public interest. But unless they also investigate actual institutions and try to change them, they are isolated from the active side of social change that is essential to their education.

Younger students can investigate problems such as water and air pollution and then inquire into the reasons for the problems. They may find a lack of appropriate legislation or a lack of monitoring and enforcement. They can help educate their own local communities. They will probably gain more understanding of the actual problems of pollution control by direct action, and they may effect some actual change. Even young children should learn to be sensitive to their physical and social environment, as part of the development process of becoming agents of social change. Participative change can begin in the earliest levels of school, as children are taught to cooperatively redesign their classroom environment and then move out into the school grounds and soon into the larger community.

By the time students are in high school they should be involved in planning social futures with respect to population, resource utilization and distribution, pollution control, and peace planning. Humanistic studies such as religion, art, and literature should be incorporated in such a way as to help students design future qualities of experience. Such exploration of alternatives will not be merely academic; it will be a prerequisite to designing the future of the broadest community that can make sense to the student at his level of development. The direction of development must be global in order for humanization to be adequate and for planning to be sufficient. Problems such as war, pollution, and resource utilization and distribution are solvable only by a global system of planning. So public interest must consist of world interest, and curricula must be transformed accordingly.

The movement toward increased student participation in the government of schools is well underway. The next priority is for faculty and students to transform subject matter so that it contributes to the transformation of the larger society. It then would become possible for schools to contribute to peace instead of war, to social justice instead of exploitation, and to ecological balance instead of ecocide.

In brief, if schools emphasized reconstructive education as it has been proposed, they would do the following:

1. Identify present trends.

2. Reexamine cultural and survival values.

3. Identify ecological parameters of choice.

4. Build alternative models of the future.

5. Identify social change priorities.

6. Participate in the implementation of plans.

7. Continuously reassess, criticize, and evaluate.

8. Move toward a global conception of man and a global basis for problem solving.

The need now is to develop an education that puts man as a species, supported by intelligence and responsibility, in charge of his own collective destiny; otherwise he will be destroyed by his old habits and institutions even while he loudly proclaims that he is free.

The Structure of Reconstructive Planning

Reconstructive planning requires information:

1. About trends, locally, nationally, and globally in relation to survival problems (war, pollution, population, resources).

2. About trends, locally, nationally, and globally in relation to social justice problems (poverty, human rights).

3. About trends in environmental quality, socially, aesthetically, and ecologically.

It requires analysis and environmental information about alternative models of the future:

1. What kinds of futures are ecologically possible? What kinds of futures are ecologically probable? (energy sources, critical pollution levels, etc.).

2. What kinds of futures are socially possible? (war systems versus peace-keeping systems, elitist versus democratic political structures, plutocracy versus socialism).

3. What kinds of environmental experience are within the range of human tolerance?

It requires aspirational models, optimum possible ties:

1. What kind of conflict management system is most desirable? (war-nation state, world law, etc.).

2. What kind of social and economic justice is most desirable? (movement toward equal political power and economic wealth or a worldwide market system?)

3. What kind of social and aesthetic factors are more desired in the planning of cities, work, recreation, and housing?

It requires transition strategies necessary to move from here to there. Such strategies need to evaluate the role of:

1. Revolution.

2. Periodic reaction to crisis.

3. Continuous participatory democracy.

4. Elitist control.

It requires action to test what appears to be the most desirable plan so that a process of feedback can be used to correct the plan continuously.

Summary

The following schema presents evolving patterns of planning . Model IV is vital to the future of man, and education must become a strong vehicle for reconstructive adaptation.

Four Planning Models

	Modes of Energy Exploitation	Levels of Planning	Adaptive Patterns
Model I	Past: Pre-industrial, agricultural, group-centered.	Planning through tradition; fixed roles. Relative order of priorities: 1. Ecological; 2. Social; 3. Economic.	Static-adaptive.
Model II	Recent: Fossil fuel, engineering-centered, resource frontier, individualistic.	Minimum planning, ad hoc, short-range, laissez-faire. Relative order of priorities: 1. Economic; 2. Social; 3. Ecological.	Expansive.

Four Planning Models (continued)

	Modes of Energy Exploitation	Levels of Planning	Adaptive Patterns
Model III	Present: Fossil fuel, atomic, engineering-centered, computer-assisted, resource crisis, semi-ecological, corporate.	Beginning use of rational economic cost/benefit formula; mixture of ad hoc and medium range; nation-centered. Relative order of priorities: 1. Economic; 2. Social (crisis adaptive); 3. Ecological (ad hoc, reactive).	Expansive-suicidal.
Model IV	Future (?): renewable energy, ecology-centered, recycling, computer-based, species-centered.	Reconstructive, integrative, anticipatory, design-centered, participatory, long- range, global. Relative order of priorities: 1. Ecological (global cost/benefit); 2. Social (global cost/benefit); 3. Economic (instrumental to above values; no economic development as an end itself).	Reconstructive-adaptive.

Notes

1. Michael Harrington, *Accidental Century* (New York: Macmillan, 1965).
2. Jean-Paul Sartre, *Existentialism and Human Emotions* (New York: Philosophical Library, 1957), p. 17; also see pp. 9-51.
3. Robert Diamond, "What Business Thinks—The Fortune 500-Yankelovich Survey," *Fortune* (February, 1970), pp. 118-19, 171-72.

Chapter Five

Planning Education and Systems Change

> *There is no alternative to the schools*
> *being an agent of social change—*
> *the choices are "what kind" serving "whom."*

This is a proposal for education to focus on teaching people to plan *the* future, as distinguished from planning *for* the future. Planning *for* the future involves adaptation to trends; planning *the* future involves systems change. Planning for the future results, paradoxically, in the destruction of the members of the species. Planning of the future requires a species-centered planning in which cooperation is not merely one more ideology but a prerequisite for survival.

It is not new to treat educational institutions as instruments of social planning. This has been done for somewhile in newly developing countries. It is new to treat education as a process which teaches people to design preferred futures and to learn to undertake their realization. In this period of history there is no alternative to fundamental systems change if the human race is to survive. However, mere survival can occur in a world that stifles human dignity and social justice. And even social justice is not sufficient; we must develop a high quality of life within our social and physical environment.

Survival, social justice, and environmental quality require participation in systems change among those who are seriously affected by the transformation. Few people, however, have learned to participate in this kind of planning. A fundamentally new education is required if human life, including education, is to survive and flourish.

Education and Social Change

Forty years ago George Counts asked whether schools should build a new social order. The question should now be restated as "Dare the School *Not* Help Build a New Social Order?" There is actually no alternative to the school becoming an agent of social change. The choice is, rather, what kind of social agent it should become, serving what purposes? Schools can: (1) intentionally reinforce the status quo; (2) unintentionally reinforce the status quo; (3) intentionally transform through intelligence and participation; and (4) transform through polarization and violence, intentionally or unintentionally.

Many educators claim to serve the third objective of transformation through intelligence and participation, while in fact they usually serve the second objective of unintentionally preserving the status quo. If Americans actually believe in intelligence and participation, we have half our work already done, yet the appropriate translation into practice is still needed.

The term *radical education* is becoming so conventional that it is now a common currency of establishment publishers. The label is often applied to that group called the "new humanists" who have interpreted both "humanism" and "radical" in the context of a development they term "counterculture." Usually radical education also involves interpersonal relationships in groups, where the aim is to develop a sense of community by means of creating a more simple and decentralized world. Though many of these "radical" advocates are actually producing variations on the old theme of Rousseauian romanticism with the nostalgic aim of recovering pre-industrial community, we must still commend them for sensing that something is fundamentally wrong with contemporary society. What they lack is any design of a future that takes sufficient account of science and technology and the need to form worldwide solutions to exponentially increasing worldwide problems. A really new and relevant "humanism" should help people control the technological juggernaught for ethical and ecological ends, a 180-degree of transformation from present trends. In the meantime, the war system not only stays intact, it becomes stronger. The gap between the rich and the poor continues within the United States, and expands even more rapidly between underdeveloped and overdeveloped countries. And the ecological basis for the support of an exponentially expanding population is increasingly undermined. Members of the countercultures know that the Gross National Product is indeed a gross product, but they seldom design effective strategies for social change. Part of the trouble, indeed, is that most proposals are far from radical enough. That is, they rarely confront problems such as analyzing the dynamics of change, problems of designing a humane and ecologically tenable world, or problems of specifying the steps necessary to make viable transitions. To confront these problems may seem like an insurmountably large order, but it has already taken extraordinary intelligence to create the planetary mess we are now in. With a vision for what needs to be done, the human race has the capacity to achieve the needed transformation.

Social Systems Change

In order to advocate the kind of "systems" change to which I have alluded, it is necessary to point out that the term "system" is commonly used in our industrial society to mean either technical system or efficiency system, neither of which alters the purpose of their operation. The Pentagon wants new weapons systems; corporations want new management systems or new production systems. The Pentagon never asks for a peace-keeping system, nor do corporations ask for new economic systems. What they do ask for are improvement of *subsystems* so that the political system will *not* change. Yet political systems are the main determiners of the future; they are the most powerful of all social systems.

There are two basically different kinds of systems: natural and social. Natural systems have formed their own process of biological interdependency. Unlike mechanical systems, they thrive on complexity and are self-healing. Most natural systems are so complex that we only understand a fraction of their processes, yet they constitute the network of the life-support system, the biosphere on which all life depends. It constitutes good planning to honor existing ecosystems. However, there is no defensible reason to adjust to existing *social* systems, especially those that are pathological. Liberal traditions have moved from old beliefs in "ethnocentrism" to a tolerance for pluralism which assumes "their way is the right way," in which all cultural systems are thus self-justifying. But such self-justification provides no basis for transforming pathological cultural systems and we need to develop plans to abolish cultural systems which support human exploitation systems and ecological self-destruct systems. To put it another way, the term "system" ordinarily involves the structure, interrelations, and procedures which produce rules for a social game that predetermine the choices that can be made, thus it loads the dice in terms of particular outcomes. There is no such thing as a predetermined social system that provides "freedom" of choice; each system provides its own "freedoms" within its own framework and excludes others.

Analysis of the way in which these systems include some outcomes and preclude others should be a basic concern of education. The need in this urgent period of history is to stop the process of reinforcing traditional social systems which exploit natural systems, and to begin the reconstruction which will permit us to adjust to natural systems and exploit possibilities in selecting alternative social systems. Our current implicit theory of "adaptation" is suicidal, for individual adjustment to pathological trends intensifies the trends instead of systematically transforming them.

Intentional social planning was considered a subversive concept in the United States until recent years. Now the central question is not whether or not there will be planning, but whether there will be an explicit or an implicit form of planning. The need is to make certain the planning is *ex*plicit and that the goals and the means are therefore sufficiently clear. We also have the choice of whether planning will include widespread participation or whether it will be elitist; whether planning will merely increase the efficiency by which to achieve present goals, or whether there will be transformation in goals involving simultaneous transformation of the meaning of "progress" and "development."

All such problems are educational problems in which the psychologically-based theories of "growth and development" also require transformation. Either the schools will teach planning in the participatory and sociological framework I urge, or elitist planning will occur by default. The danger is that planning will be planning *for* the future which does not transform basic systems. Today's treatment of planning is inundated with expansive, predictive, reinforcing planning, while few educators as yet understand the alternative of transformational, participatory, systemic planning.

The Moral Foundations of Planning

If the future is to serve human life, planning theory must also be based upon moral presuppositions. Some forms of planning, such as market place capitalism, presume that good social results can come from bad motives, but the purpose of good planning is to increase direction rather than to find consolation in occasional fortuitous accidents. Humanistic planning gives central consideration to *quality* of life. The principle of "the worth and dignity of the human person," which is widely acknowledged in principle if not in practice, could be used to produce remarkable political and economic transformation. But it often competes with a rival principal, individual "freedom of choice." If "freedom of choice" is the first principle and "the worth of the individual" is a second-order principle, we can justify the freedom of the market place as the accepted basis for economic distribution. But if human worth is a central moral presupposition, then we have a principle of fundamental equality by which the economic system should be designed to serve *human* needs no matter what race, sex, lifestyle, creed, or wealth of one's parents. This would constitute a radical change in the American economic system and others based on capitalist principles.

The Myth of Neutralism

Much education, particularly higher education, has assumed that goals should be intellectually centered rather than morally centered. When there are no social commitments for which intelligence should be selectively used, intelligence becomes both a means and an end, and intellectual technique does serve goals—those of the established political order. The illusion of objectivity is a useful device for providing moral consolation to academicians and for keeping the dominant social systems intact. This is one form of cooperation to be sure, but certainly not the kind I am advocating.

The neutralist myth is so pervasive that most social studies education, parading as "the new social studies," is based on "inquiry method" without explicit presuppositions for what it is we need to inquire into. This method tends to assume that the desirability of war, poverty, or ecocide is to be always treated as an open question—an assumption tantamount to medical schools spending their time inquiring into the question of the desirability of sickness rather than the legitimate moral question of how medical education can get on with the biased task of finding ways of preventing and curing sickness. To be neutral about the value of human life is an *academic* sickness and just as spurious. The higher learning should be against war, poverty, ecocide, and racism in the same sense that the medical school is against sickness, for these are anti-human systems.

Value commitment means some form of partiality, the alternative being *indifference,* which is itself *not* impartial. So the real question is: What kind of partiality is most defensible? The answer is affirmation of human life and the political systems necessary to the kind of law, order, and justice that would serve a more life-affirming and equitable future. Schools are not invariably and certainly not explicitly precommitted to the elimination of war, poverty, and ecocide. If they were, they would be designing the steps which would substitute life-affirming systems.

Defensible partiality requires that we maximize public interest in contrast with special interest. Public interest which is global and based on ethical humanism becomes equivalent to world interest. When these moral presuppositions are translated into curricular terms, education is centered around the process of using knowledge to teach people to design the transition steps necessary to help achieve world-oriented goals. World goals can be defined as those which produce world community by developing systems which: (1) sustain human life; (2) provide maximum social justice; and (3) involve collective participation in determining and improving the *quality* of life.

A Curricular Model

The following model provides an outline of a curriculum theory based on these principles. Since the dynamics of current world change threaten human survival through war, overpopulation, pollution, and resource depletion, we can stipulate the required elements of a survival system. Since economic maldistribution and basic human rights maldistribution defeat the goal of social justice, we can stipulate the elements of a social-justice system. Since the quality of environment and human experience is now only a by-product of a world that gives accidental attention to the design of environmental quality, we can stipulate the elements of a society that try to improve the quality of experience. In brief, the school should become an instrument for teaching planning, which in turn helps to effect the transformation from an inadequate, even pathological, present toward clearly committed goals which are necessary for human survival, social justice, and a better quality of life.

Goals at the top of the list are somewhat specifically definable, but there also needs to be participation in defining goals of social justice and environmental quality more precisely. Schools using this model should help students to share in effecting population stabilization, in designing the transition from a war system to a peace-keeping system, and in planning ways of developing ecological stability. Transformations such as these would require change in lifestyle and public policy. To put it another way, students would be learning to use intelligence to invent channels to effect the transition from a bitter Malthusian world of ruthless struggle to survive amidst scarcity of resources and overabundance of population to a post-Malthusian world in which ecological stability and high levels of environmental quality are planned and shared, instead of waiting for "nature" to plan by means of the violence and death of "positive checks."

An Outline of Systems Change

From   *Toward*

1. Survival
a. population expansion   population stabilization
b. a war system   a peace-keeping system
c. pollution of the biosphere   termination of pollution
d. waste of natural resources   conservation-recycling

2. Social Justice
a. economic disparity   economic equality
b. violations of human rights   equal human rights

3. Environmental Quality
a. an ugly environment   a beautiful environment
b. alienation, social disintegration social ecology, community

Though the general goals of transition planning would be "given," the means of achieving them would be "open." We now know that survival requires a "steady-state" recycling economic system in global ecological equilibrium instead of the current expanding economic system based on GNP. The gross national product approach ignores the inevitable and disastrous conflict between infinite expansion and a finite world. Education should contribute to effecting the transition in public policy and lifestyle to a steady-state system.

Planning Methodology

To design the future requires baseline information about local, national, and global social and ecological trends. It also requires models of ecologically possible futures, as distinguished from science fiction models. Baseline trends and models of possible futures require specialists to assure empirical accuracy and logical connections between variables. But identification of preferred futures requires the judgment of those who will experience that future. Unless alternatives acquire clarity of meaning in experiential terms, the lifeless symbols of trends charts such as those in *The Limits of Growth*[1] will fail unless there is more sensitivity to the content of meaningful choices. Planning should utilize, too, a full range of talents in the natural and social sciences as well as in the humanities. Policy analysis is a new discipline, and prescriptive policy analysis is even newer. The publicizing of planning can democratize the process of social change, requiring not only new responsibilities for education, but new ways to make unrealized, even unexperienced, qualities of life sufficiently real so that meaningful choices can be determined for selecting or rejecting such a future.

In addition, there should be continuous connection between theory and practice so that people can engage in effective political activity leading to change toward futures. Schools now commit the fallacy of separating theory and practice, under the claim of keeping education intellectually pure and avoiding the danger of turning education into a propaganda instrument for special interest groups. What makes education an instrument of special interest groups is not the connection of theory and practice, but the failure to create an adequate theory of public interest. When planning is a *public* activity, based on a theory of social needs with established legitimate boundaries of special interests, the planning process substitutes an integrated political-educational *system* for the factional laissez-faire "pluralism" of conventional "liberal" politics. Law and justice replace the covert manipulation of lobbies and spoils systems. Economic power is constrained by public law. Community replaces society.

Among the numerous obstacles to transforming young Americans into cooperative citizens is the atomistic individualism that encourages the belief that self-realization is Dionysian, personal, and subjective. The democratization of planning requires a social commitment to the development of "persons," not merely "individuals." There is less obstacle to this concept in Eastern thought than in Western, where the image of man is rooted in genetic, political, and religious conceptions of anarchism, and competitive individualism is the approved mythology justifying varieties of Social Darwinism. When schools encourage competitive grades, team rivalry, and curriculum tracking to sort and cull under the belief that excellence will come to the top and provide a "natural" leadership pool, they are in fact perpetuating this Western ideology.

Alienated minority groups have learned to stop this group fragmentation game by developing ethnic group identity. The method is ethnocentric and atomizes the larger society, but it does begin to stress *social* self-realization, and it does provide a foundation for widening the base and integrating human relations into large patterns. Part of our integration strategy could be to focus on solutions to *common* human problems, requiring the development of highly systemic subject matter such as global ecology. This would help create a new common set of cultural values, as educational subject matter focused on war systems, world poverty systems, political power structures, and the way culture shapes reality and modifies the future.

New Foundations of Education

Appropriate signs of needed change in the foundations of education should include the "ecological foundations of education," along with such specializations as "the thermodynamic foundations of education." Courses on world order should become commonplace, and curriculum and instruction should be based on planning theory and a new conception of "growth and development."

The social and philosophical foundations of education should retool and create systems change theory. The challenge is considerable, for we live in a society that has virtually no understanding of systems change. Both American political parties were dedicated in their 1972 party platforms to the elimination of the Vietnam war. Neither was dedicated nor even gave recognition to the elimination of the *war system* itself. Yet schools continue to develop preatomic citizens as irresponsibly as the mother who teaches her child about the dangers of cars while letting him run across the freeway.

The current "energy crisis" is seen as an American problem requiring *administrative* changes in quotas, prices, and tax structures. The real crisis is not understood, for it is based on the failure to build civilization on renewable resources, exploiting the stored non-renewable resources created in ancient times for an orgy of consumption which disregards future generations and even most of the present world population. Problems of environment, war, and poverty are now defined so they are subject only to band-aid treatment, confusing a minor wound with cancer. The foundations of education should shift from band-aid treatment to integrated planning and systems substitution.

This new education should teach people to guide social change, but it should begin with the more immediate, short-range problems of planning close to the student's experience. Such firsthand projects as redesigning a single classroom could be the microcosm of collective environment planning. Increasingly, too, there should be participation in planning curricula and in political control of the school, while expanding from the local community toward larger political systems. Meanwhile, democratic commitments should emphasize more equalitarian views of social and political development as students begin to design optimum economic distribution ratios and changes in public policy as these are required to plan social transformation. Law should be conceived as a potential instrument of value realization, instead of an instrument for supporting the present power structure. On a higher intellectual-affective level, the curricula should confront similar transformation in order to identify fresh, novel contributions to better ways of life. All the professions—including medicine, law, architecture, religion—should require equally qualitative transformation. Agriculture, engineering, art, physical education—all need to be self-conscious about the way in which they have contributed to reinforcement of the old order and the way in which their own transformation becomes part of the process of changing culture and history.

Schools are currently discovering that traditional services to industrial society are declining in social value. The market system is adding teachers to lists of the unemployed, and so teachers like others acquire a vested interest of their own in planning a world where people are no longer bought and sold like commodities. We now need to design creative new forms of work that are ecologically responsible, satisfying, educational, and socially valuable. Then we should organize types of political action that are necessary to produce such changes. If teachers assume that readjustments in the local tax base will cure the unemployment problem that they now share, they are really revealing how uneducated they are. The problem has to do largely with *national priorities*. The unemployed art teacher needs to see the connection between the war system and the welfare system he relies on.

Two Fundamental Principles

No principle is more important to ecological planning than what is called "The Tragedy of the Commons," a parable described by Garrett Hardin. The story is about farmers who each have enough cows to survive on the common grazing area. Then one farmer decided to add to his profit by getting another cow, recognizing that his action makes only an incremental demand on the limited grazing land, but adds considerably to his own profit. The other farmers are no less adept at maximizing their advantages, and the scenario predetermines the outcome—overgrazing of the land, dead cows, and tragedy to the village. In our global village the parable equally applies. Basically this illustrates the principle of a system that permits and encourages only unilateral choice and leads to the destruction of nonrenewable resources. It also illustrates that common control of the common, finite, life-support system is one prerequisite to survival, not merely one more comparative ideology. It illustrates why individual, corporate, and national autonomy are pre-ecological concepts. It establishes one basic consideration for political systems design.

"Structural violence" is a principle of comparable importance in order to plan social justice. We are already familiar with the direct violence that destroys us through war and homicide. But structural violence destroys through exploitation of one group by another. Social structures cause some to do violence to others through political and economic power that is vertical and hierarchical. Its symptoms are sometimes only discoverable by such statistical studies as differential mortality rates, differential illness rates, and differential levels of optimism and mental health. Structural violence plagues the present world order and is endemic in various degrees within all countries. From what we know it seems minimal to post-revolutionary China, and this is one of the reasons why Cuba's type of socialism is likely to be especially attractive to newly developing countries. Maldistribution of wealth is endemic in the American system, and most of the economic planning devices that the West has used such as "free trade," "aid," "development," and the "multi-national corporation" are revealing themselves to be instruments of structural violence traveling incognito.

Modern tyranny is seldom perpetrated by tyrants; far more often it is perpetrated by well intentioned members of the inherited order. Without the "structural violence" concept, we will not be able to analyze social systems for much of anything except their more obvious exploitations. This is one of the reasons why many of the young are cynical about voting. They have seen how elections have produced new actors who produce the same old results. Without understanding the concept of structural violence, they presume that political action is useless; thereby they perpetuate *both* the existing structure *and* its actors.

Obstacles

Planning education should be based on realistic assumptions about the obstacles endemic in the old order. (Not all aspects of the old order need changing; some things are changing that need to be retained.) The old order includes the following characteristics, which serve as elements of a secular religion that produce negative, self-fulfilling prophesies, which reinforce predetermined images of human capacity, guide change, and constitute a hidden political agenda:

1. *Technofanaticism:* This involves a faith in engineering rather than ecology. It treats engineering as a way of life, forming the social principles that determine public policy, therefore (a) whatever is technologically possible ought to be done, and (b) everything has a technological solution. The two principles give us NASA, SSTs, ICBMs, anti-ballistic missiles, anti-anti-ballistic missiles, anti-anti-anti-ballistic missiles, plus much of the burgeoning creativity that we proudly categorize under American "know-how."

2. *Supranaturalism:* Man is above nature, not a partner of nature; as in Genesis, he is here to "multiply and subdue the earth." He is a planetary conquistador, and exploitation of planet Earth is his destiny and his right, divine or otherwise.

3. *Unilateral Individualism:* Under this metaphysics of social atomism, individuals are unique, and their uniqueness is given by nature or God. Identity means separateness. Autonomy is good; community and law are bad. Corporations have a God-given right to choose their own destiny.

4. *Capitalism:* Economics should be directed by profit-making and, if possible, the appearance of competition. Quantitative acquisition and production of goods and services is an end in itself. The market place is the central instrument for planning and creating the future. Freedom means the assurance of the continuation of profit-making opportunity.

5. *Determinism:* The forces of change are irrevocable and outside the power of people. People cannot create the future, they can only predict it. Science should be used to anticipate change. The basic systems that determine change are not man-made games but are part of the nature of reality, whether the systems are natural or social.

Though the above obstacles are classified separately, they are integral faith components of a way of life, premises of the theology of the old order. Teachers should help students to examine these assumptions in the context of the central problems of this period of human history. The old order continues partly because we have given so little philosophical examination to the presuppositions on which it is based.

The Myth of Unilateral Responsibility

I do not wish to suggest that intellectual examination of the inadequacy of old systems is sufficient. What is urgent is *systems substitution,* with carefully planned transitions that do not threaten people with loss of jobs. The current administration helps prevent necessary change by keeping a high unemployment level and by providing no guarantee of jobs when industries receive cutbacks in funds. When the game is played this way, the polls will reveal support of such obsolete policy as high levels of military spending.

Similarly, people are not willing to abandon their automobiles when there is no other guaranteed substitution for adequate transportation. Nor will they support unilateral disarmament without a plan simultaneously to phase in an international system of national defense. Neither will they unilaterally distribute their money to the poor without a just and equal policy for wealth and income redistribution. Corporation presidents admit that they do not intend to take unilateral responsibility for curtailing the pollution of their factories unless they are compelled to do so by national legislation. People are not naturally greedy, they become greedy or civilized depending on what the system calls for.

Reliance on unilateral responsibility without systems change is therefore one of the myths supporting the old order. It is reinforced by the schools when they fail to teach integrated systemic planning. Our current world is created *ad hoc,* by chance, by the dynamics of technology and population expansion, and by unrepresentative portions of the human race such as corporations, political elites, and wealthy nations. The principle of integrated planning of the future by people for people is probably the most radical theory of education that schools could use. It seems also to be the most civilized, just, and lawful.

Conclusions

To summarize more specifically, I am proposing an education that would:

1. focus on man as a social, political, ecological, and creating being;

2. be futuristic in designing social change;

3. use planning education as the core of the curriculum;

4. develop an ecological consciousness and conscience;
5. connect theory and practice, combining design *and* participation in social change;

6. treat economic systems as means to serve social and ecological goals;

7. encourage identity as expanding community levels, from local to global;

8. encourage development of a species-centered world interest planning guided by conceptions of politics, law, and morality which are directed toward building global institutions;

9. identify the dynamics of current change, ecologically possible futures, and design *preferred* collective futures;

10. maximize the values of survival, social justice, and environmental quality, giving priority in that order;

11. illuminate the future consequences of present alternative choices;

12. help create a new theory of human development and political development based on the way institutions, knowl-

edge, and technology should serve to improve the common quality of experience;

13. treat the development of human community as a central value of the selection of educational experience.

We live in a pre-Malthusian, pre-ecological, pre-atomic social and political order, and yet the minimum requirements for survival require transformation to a post-Malthusian, ecologically based, post-atomic world which manages technological powers, serves human needs equitably, and averts World War III. Since we are living in an age of pathological self-destruct systems, transformation requires a radical level of consciousness and therefore a radical kind of education. The minimal responsibility of such an education would include learning to help design and effect the transition. For schools to be "neutral" about such questions as whether we need a war system or a peace-keeping system, population stability or continual expansion, pollution or clean air is both absurd and immoral. In short, the primary focus of education should be toward the design and realization of transition steps that transform pathological systems into life-affirming systems.

Note

1. Donella H. Meadows et al., *The Limits to Growth* (New York: Universe Books, 1972).

Chapter Six

Universities and Social Priorities

> *The university should be the central intellectual agency for identifying systemic problems of society and alternative solutions.*

Universities, like the American political-economic system, are without an explicit set of social priorities. Procedures exist for deciding who gets what, but the procedures have no necessary connection with social needs. Instead, the priorities of universities are responses to faculty politics, fragmented pressures from business, legislatures (in public institutions) and Boards of Regents, the market for courses, and the bits and pieces of "soft" money available through public and private grants.

Individual instructors may help students analyze social needs, but the enormous power of universities to channel human resources and to help create the future is done without a guiding theory of social priorities. Universities have been under pressure to plan, but their responses are based on clarifying goals and providing better organization of purposes. The purposes, however, continue to be the same.

Universities characterize themselves as unique places in American society where rational and theoretical processes can flourish, and they also claim to be "humanistic." Yet the very fact that universities have no rationale for a *social* mission illuminates the central pathology of American higher education. The dominant official ideology is a mixture of the belief that knowledge is an end in itself and that it should serve the individual student, while in fact it usually serves to retain the power structure of the larger society.

Yet American universities are not ordinarily involved in direct conspiratorial collusion with the wealthy and the powerful. Rather most members of the faculty and administration actually believe they are progressive agents of social change. But by fragmenting knowledge, equating knowledge with one's academic discipline, separating theory from practice, accepting individual interests and the drift of market demand as the basis for program development, the university becomes a major reinforcer of liberal capitalism.

Professors respond to social problems mainly by being ready to undertake band-aid research to put a finger in the economic or political dike or to teach courses that describe problems but avoid solutions. Even the word "humanities" has such a vague meaning that it is readily available to classify all courses other than social science, natural science, or the professions as inherently humanizing. Humanities fields such as philosophy have usually organized themselves to promote a sterile intellectual imperialism that separates philosophy from the problems of life and requires the students to enter an intellectual order that treats philosophy as an end in itself, adding to the ethical paralysis to which other largely separatist orders, such as history, anthropology, and even the arts, usually contribute.

In a responsible university, ethics would be supreme, but the ethics would be functional and tied with human relations and public planning. In a fragmented society, the university often only adds to the student's alienation from the human community because information and concepts are usually separated from the ethical problems and the social planning imperatives of our age.

Salvation by Growth

The university has saved itself from its own irrelevance in the same way as has the larger society. Expansion in the name of growth has provided a larger pie and some opportunity for new groups to get a piece of the action of the modern "multiversity." But this Keynesian "growth" process occurs mainly when hot or cold wars contribute to American "prosperity." In recent years the university has experienced the slow-growth and no-growth effects of the economic stagnation which came in the wake of Vietnam and the increased price of Arab oil. During this slow period, various forms of accountability have kept faculty and administration busy doing detailed bookkeeping, budgeting, and program planning as a basis for justifying the survival of the competing sub-units. Because accountability was used without a theory of responsibility, an enormous waste of money, time, and human resources occurred. If the energy that has gone into these bookkeeping games had gone into creating a socially responsible university, a revolution in higher education could have occurred. But a structurally fragmented university with individualistic faculty who treat their academic freedom more as a personal right than as a social obligation instead moved politics in the same direction as American workers in the 1930—unions and collective bargaining developed, but nothing resembling an intellectual community with responsible social goals resulted. As with the workers of the 1930s, the threats produced a retention of the same social goals with better forms of personal job security.

Opportunities Within Crisis

But crisis can be an opportunity to transform social goals. When people come together they can reassess the purposes of their institution and help set it straight. Analysis of the problems of the new social context and developing world problems provides a basis for transforming institutional obsolescence. Universities could provide an example of people in control of institutions, whereas the usual relationship is for institutions to control people. The central intellectual error is to concentrate on the *internal* problems of the university rather than the *external* problems of the larger society. This ethnocentrism treats the university as an end in itself and cripples its social utility.

The university is especially vulnerable to outside pressures when it does not know what it ought to be doing. The university should be the central intellectual agency for identifying the systemic problems of people. By giving priority to human potential, social justice, and the quality of life, the university could transform knowledge into a powerful social instrument for ordering priorities and planning social change. This would constitute an epistemological revolution.

From Expedience and Habit to Social Ethics

The central characteristic of such education is that it would focus on applied ethics, which extend ethics beyond the interpersonal level, typical of liberal ideology, into the ethics of institutions and organized systems of power. Therefore economic planning, political planning, health planning, employment planning, environmental planning, and war prevention planning would be typical of central concerns. Since human beings are of central importance—whatever race, creed, or sex—more economic justice, more equal political rights, more opportunity to develop as human beings, and avoidance of environmental irreversibility become examples of the *outcome goals* to which universities should be dedicated.

In such a university science serves society rather than merely other scientists. The university becomes a leader of responsible social change rather than the expedient follower of a confused world with many obsolete institutions.

Universities should not devote all their energies to social needs, but they should have central priorities. Priority Number 1 should include the kinds of ethical-social-needs-planning listed above. Priority Number 2 could include continuation of some of the more useful aspects of discipline-centered academic objectives. And everything else could be Priority Number 3. Hiring, firing, budget development, facilities construction, and program development would then be guided by a responsible rationale.

The Myth of Neutrality

Professors are, to their credit, sensitive about the kind of authoritarian indoctrination they have seen in church schools and in nationalistic and totalitarian institutions. However, they often come to the fallacious conclusion that if authoritarian indoctrination is avoided, and if factual information is used, there is no bias. Therefore, a prevailing ideology supports the mythology that if a data base is used, and if quantitative methods are used, and if logical inferences are accurate, then bias is avoided. The frames of reference and principles of selectivity underlying all research and inquiry are like icebergs, and only the tips are usually seen.

A similar form of thought was used for years in American foreign policy—avoid totalitarian communism and you will be serving the cause of freedom and truth. Many university Ph.D.s were ready to serve the cause when the money was available. And educational experiments were producing "free," permissive, nondirected programs that gave students the opportunity to drift in the name of freedom. "Inquiry methods" still dominate high school social studies, without a theory of what should be inquired into nor with any assumptions about the moral goals of inquiry. The ethical baby went out in the bath of personal preference.

Selectivity and bias is a part of the human condition that is best handled by comparing the preferability of frames of reference rather than denying preference in the name of objectivity. Selection of information, texts, courses, and instructors involves inclusion and exclusion. The particular problems, hypotheses, and presuppositions that are used are never inclusive of everything, and the commonplace failure to prepare students to understand and to try to help solve the central problems of our age is hardly a neutral stance. Formal education is highly political, whether or not its ideology is intentional.

Some applied areas have come to terms with some key elements of the neutrality myth. Medical and public health schools operate in support of the values of health instead of illness and never give equal time to the proponents of illness. Yet by fragmenting medicine and social-needs economics, medical schools usually ignore the problem of distribution, which has negative moral consequences.

Colleges of engineering have usually been ready to sell their technical skill to any source willing to pay for it. Law schools often produce good technicians who can practice within the law that exists, but neither as lawyers nor as the politicians they often become do they usually treat law as an invention that needs to be concerned centrally with justice. The professions are as adrift as the university itself, responding mainly to the "real" world of jobs, status, power, and money within the peculiar kind of democratic capitalism that has developed in the United States.

When there is a failure to distinguish between what is and what

:atus quo and the descriptive use of knowledge are
:tic." Without social needs priorities the university
ıre ROTC and yet have no courses in disarmament.
 ..υ ıearn about the war system, the poverty system, and the
ecocide system, they often do so within the descriptive mode, and they
take on an informed cynicism because they have learned to separate
theory from practice and analysis from ethics. Their instructors often
give them many reasons why nothing can be done. They understand
the past and the present but they have been taught to do nothing about
the future.

What is needed is a clear and consistent bias on the part of
universities *for* human rights and *against* war, poverty, and ecocide.
Though such a stand requires considerable clarification of the goals
and exploration of a variety of transition steps, the importance of such
a stand is that it legitimizes instrumental uses of knowledge to serve
explicit social goals and channel human energy instead of diffusing it.
Currently universities avoid questions of social ethics and presume
that if knowledge is created and diffused it will serve society, whereas
it usually just retains the current structure of power. Professors of
economics are usually professors of capitalist economics, though I
know of none who uses such truth in advertising.

The liberal commitment to individualism compounds the problem
by assigning sovereign axiological authority to each person. This
places personal preference over ethical standards and instead of
focusing on our obligations to each other as human beings, personal
desires are given as much free reign in the university as in the larger
economy. Students collect information and course grades for their own
use to provide better competitive advantage in the economic system.

But when the faculty are imaginative enough to break through the
pattern, some remarkable things happen. Instead of being a historian
who paralyzes students with a false sense of determinism or a
disconnected variety of events, the past serves as a lesson. When
people learned to live in peace, the reasons are studied; when war
occurred the question "what should have been done that was not done"
becomes relevant.

Business courses, properly taught, become ways to organize
responsible economic transactions instead of ways to obtain profit
whatever the consequences. Schools of agriculture and forestry, which
usually ally with business to apply the technology of industry to

economic objectives, start serving ways of increasing equitable nutrition, stabilizing ecosystems and watersheds, and protecting the breeding grounds of fish. And teachers of teachers in schools of education shift from their usual role as conveyor belt suppliers of teachers and principals for the schools to educators who are increasing public understanding of social change and alternative futures.

The Ethical Core

In place of the usual "liberal arts" core, which typically serves to herd undergraduates into every department's courses to provide economic survival for the departments, I propose the following "core":

1. One aspect will be concerned with understanding the world and where it is going. This is a time dimension which consists of descriptive knowledge, past—present—the future, if trends continue.

2. These base line trends will then be subject to the ethical question "What ought to be?" The current emerging future will then be contrasted with other alternatives and assessed on the basis of ethical preferability. Ethical preferability is not the same as personal preferability, it is rather the obligation toward others because they are human beings, and "justice" is on eof the basic ethical values.

3. Preferred futures should be based both on personal behavior and the transformation of basic institutions such as political and economic systems. Transformation strategies should therefore be based largely on systems planning.

4. Theory and practice should be related so that concepts are not disconnected from their use, therefore learning should involve direct work in communities, and implementation of plans should require social action.

The primary set of problems should be those for which the most serious consequences are likely to develop, affecting survival, justice, and quality of life. Topics such as population, resources, pollution, war, economic distribution, community, and human rights would be among the central considerations.

Some *a priori* decisions can be made for preferred outcomes. Since the entire process focuses centrally on the principle of the worth and dignity of the person, we know some things which are *categorically* undesirable: for example, ecological changes which produce the kinds of irreversibility that close options and destroys long-run carrying capacity, and premature death and unnecessary human suffering caused by disease, war, starvation, and torture.

Similarly, there are a priori categories of desirability, such as reductions of political, economic, and educational inequality; improved common quality of life involving increased quality of life-support systems; better public information; better appreciations; better health; more community cooperation; more and better esthetic experience; work that contributes to socially useful and environmentally responsible outcomes; and a planned balance between community and autonomy.

Such a liberal education is global and human rights-centered, yet the sequence of learning would require beginning where a person is, psychologically and culturally, so that the new learning would be developmental and meaningful. But the purpose of such education would be to help people create a reality to which none of us have been accustomed, for it would involve designing the future and helping create it. Since learning would combine knowing and doing, theory building would be a highly practical process which guides action, and action would involve control of institutions and our own behavior so that there is real progress toward an improved common quality of life.

This kind of involvement in socio-political change is the most powerful form of psychological therapy. Current liberal capitalism creates a morass of subjectivism and alienation that produces escapism through drugs and aggression, through rape and other forms of violence toward others, the self, and nature. Participation in the development of responsibility community would reduce the drift and the schizoid quality of American life which is endemic on the American campus.

Summary and Conclusion

The essential steps toward creating a responsible university are to:

1. Treat the university as a resource allocation institution that helps create the future through admission procedures for students and faculty and through course-program control.

2. Shift the university toward using knowledge to serve human rights. Human rights are global, supra-national, and belong to present and future generations. Serving future rights includes keeping ecosystems intact by avoiding irreversibility, and it involves institutionalizing principles of fairness in the global use of resources.

3. Teach people to plan social change by guiding economic and political policy toward human needs-centered outcomes.

4. Transform the structural obsolescence which now makes the university largely an expensive reinforcer of social fragmentation, economic inequality, and technofanaticism. Apply the new systems knowledge to social design and human needs, using the university as a leadership institution to move away from global annihilation and structural exploitation toward a new human-global order.

5. If no such basic change is presumed to be feasible, consider the possibility that the university may deserve to be abandoned or to disintegrate because of its own social disutility.

Chapter Seven

Reconstructing Social Science

*In an age of planetary ecocide
and massive poverty, social sciences
have a major responsibility still unrealized.*

Jean Mayer, President of Tufts University, points out that, "If war breaks out in the next 20 to 30 years, it will be the students of today's teachers who start it." Social sciences have a special role as major contributors to the knowledge which helps people shape public policy and direct the future—part of the foundations of democracy.

Autocratic and totalitarian societies recognize that the social sciences can be sufficiently dangerous to arbitrary power so that they are never stressed and are often prohibited. However, open democratic societies such as the United States do not make use of the potentials of social science. Public ability to understand social phenomena and alternatives to major social issues is so pathetically underdeveloped that media games can quite easily manipulate the general public through methods that insult the intelligence of socially educated citizenry.

The solution involves not simply more of the same, but transformation in the content and the uses of social sciences: from laissez-faire to social issue-centered, from mere description to problem solving, from neutrality to social ethics, from fragmentation to integrated social science. To paraphrase E. F. Schumaker, we need social science "as if people mattered." Social science should not be only *about* people, but *for* people, so that people can be in charge of the human future. The future is now essentially out of control.

From Neutrality to Ethics

Probably the most corrupting assumption in social science is to equate objectivity with neutrality, which presumes that value judgments necessarily distort truth. This error encourages data and information servility, as though facts were the real truth.

The number of problems and hypotheses that can be selected for research are infinite, and the only way in which human energy can be used to cull the important from the trivial is to make value judgments, preferably for the probable social usefulness of the inquiry. If such usefulness is connected to an explicit theory of the kinds of knowledge which are of most social worth, this selective rationale can itself be subject to criticism. Excessive empiricism and the laissez-faire freedom to be nonaccountable can then be avoided.

Selectivity always occurs, even if the choice is to avoid value accountability by rolling the dice. Social science research and teaching consists of the finite use of resources to develop various kinds of power that bear on the human future. What is conspicuous by its omission is rational-ethical persuasion among social scientists to argue for a philosophy and theory of importance. And if "importance" is ethics based "as if people mattered," the meta principle of value— *the worth and dignity of the human person*—would be at the center of ethical consideration. This process "objectifies" value selection in the social sciences so that selectivity is not a matter of personal, subjective bias. It is a matter of social philosophy which responds to human considerations in this period of history. It is poker played on top of the table instead of under the table as it is now usually played.

People in applied sciences, working in the same university, have no problem with bias in favor of human life. Public Health is not balanced with a School of Public Sickness nor are Humanities programs "balanced" with inhumanities programs. But there is a curious ambivalence in the social sciences when they ally themselves with Nineteenth Century physical sciences, a tradition that still persists. This tradition of a separate objective *truth* encourages analysis and description without an ethical-philosophical-global basis for the selection of the problem and also avoids *obligation for offering solutions for such problems.* "Description" as method is very safe when it is divorced from prescription, and the amount of descriptive social information that can be used for teaching and for conferences and for books is infinite. Geologists work with resources that are finite. Social scientists have an epistemological basis for permanent full employment, as long as they define "a problem" in linguistic terms rather than in terms of social conditions. Then a "problem" will be recognized because it has a question mark after it, not because it is a real social problem.

The failure to develop ethics-centered, solution-oriented social science reduces its social value. And it creates pessimism among students if they are exposed to disconnected facts and dilemmas about the human condition but are not shown alternatives.

A Solution Model

Let us examine what social science might be, based on the following time categories: *was, is, will be like based on trends, can be, ought to be,* and *how (transition).* Such a matrix would permit an integrated, ethics-centered social science.

Was

We need first to distinguish between positive and negative causality. A historian will typically identify antecedent conditions that were in the system (positive) as central causes to explain, for example, what caused a particular war.

What was *lacking* that could have prevented the war can be called negative causality. Using "negative causality" gives recognition to the fact that social institutions are humanly invented, can be transformed, and provide humans with opportunities to shape the future and create history. Enforceable world law might be an example of negative causality, because its *lack* could be considered the major cause of the war. It is "negative" because it was not there, though it could have been. This approach to history permits us to consider how to create a better "history" from here on.

Is

Is can be treated similar to *Was*. Descriptive sociology and "realism" implicitly equates what is with what ought to be. We may learn that societies are vertically stratified, but until we explore feasible and desirable alternatives we cannot decide whether this is an inevitable structure of dominance or an example of structural exploitation. When it is recognized that unemployment is not necessary and distribution ratios can be substantially altered (by the use of negative causality), we no longer have a basis for concluding that *what is equals what ought to be,* where description is prescription. Mere descriptive sociology leads to "conservatism" in the worst sense of the word.

Trends

We have now gone from what *was* to what *is* and leaning heavily on description we can use a temporal trajectory to identify where we are going—such as population trends, resource, poverty, global ecocide trends. Trend forecast as it bears on human rights gives us the basis for identifying issues. If trends are encouraging, there is no issue. If they are not, we have a basis for planned social change.

Can Be

What *can be* defines possibilities. In the matter of Star Wars, we have a highly technical question of whether it can work as an effective defense. In the matter of world law, the question of technical feasibility is also a first consideration so that we can talk about a possible future rather than a fantasy future.

Ought To Be

There is no need to give serious attention to an alternative future unless a feasible alternative is *desirable*. If it is, it is a candidate for *what ought to be.* Desirability requires consideration of human rights. Notice that a "clean and healthful environment" ought to be a *right,* whereas polluting is not. The "common heritage of nonrenewable resources" should be a *right* of future generations, whereas making window frames from old-growth lumber is not.

Transition

Tying human rights into the "ought to be" equation builds up the list of high-priority social goals. Transition steps are next. Currently the transformation from an arms race and a militarized economy into disarmament, economic conversion, and an international common security system needs to be given widespread attention. Transition may require integration with other objectives (such as employment rights, ecological, and social justice objectives).

The above model constitutes a framework for public policy and planning and needs contributions from all of the social sciences. Notice that I have not been separating social science fields. Rather I have tried to offer a basis for ethically responsible integration of social science. Expertise from any person or any area should be welcome. We see this diverse application of frames of reference in interdisciplinary fields such as "peace studies" and "environmental studies." (These are now "tolerated" fields of low status for promotion and tenure, while the mainstream areas, which incorporate the most obsolescence, are "solid" high-status areas.)

The Current Trap

Each generation of Ph.D.s is inducted into the dominant culture, because there is no process to evaluate alternatives for reconstructing the tradition. Like the military-industrial complex, the system is highly self-perpetuating. How can one be wrong when it "works" for tenure, promotion, and publication? And how can the students know that something is wrong when no one helps them know what the alternatives are? And how can the public know that something is wrong when a degree from college still buys the higher paying jobs?

The current social science game reinforces the larger culture and the economic and political system. Information rather than ideas is stressed, technician-oriented pseudo-neutrality is rewarded, and any effort to make a better world is likely to be based on short-range, band-aid proposals that ignore structural change and make sure the larger society has no integrating long-range goals. "Social problems" are finally treated by mop-up crews learning their trade in professional colleges such as Social Work, Planning, Forestry, Agriculture, Law, and Medicine. Typical theory in these areas doesn't provide students with a basis for knowing whether they are dealing with causes or symptoms.

Whereas European social science is directed more toward structural analysis and grand theory, the American penchant is for description and information storage, so structural and systemic aspects of social systems are neglected. American economics is usually not taught as political-economics, which in practice it always is, and so students in economics classes and later in schools of business think the problems they deal with are economic problems, rather than problems of capitalistic economics. Myopic fragmentation reaches its zenith in mainstream economics and provides a powerful force for perpetuating the structure of dominance in the name of laws of economics. Students are taught to conform to deterministic forces and to get ahead by understanding them and using them for their personal "success." This provides work for psychiatrists, social workers, police forces, military occupiers of third-world countries, and specialists in real estate development.

There are many exceptions in academia to what I have outlined. Many remarkable people have chosen to reconstruct their teaching and research "as though people were important," but even they are never, in my experience, involved in developing socially responsible colleges and universities guided by social priorities based on human needs.

Robert Hutchins thought of the universities as "education for hire" rather than higher education. And recently Allan Bloom has been able to identify the ethical vacuum in higher education and make a case for "nihilism," though his proposed alternative is disconnected from the pressing social issues of our time. Lacking social goals, our colleges and universities must fall back on expedient responses to political pressures when carrots are dangled, justifying research for the Pentagon or business, using applied sciences for a stronger, competitive America.

Teaching and research should not be nationalistic. A university should strive for universality, and an education should be mainly for socially-responsible living, whereas making a living in our current society is mainly a matter of training. In an age of planetary ecocide and massive poverty, the social sciences have a key role, but without reconsideration of their social potential they may continue to make too little difference in a world where trends are ominous though the human potential for reconstructing social institutions has been barely tapped.

Chapter Eight

Toward
an Ecological Perspective
in Education

> **Our pre-ecological politics
> needs to shift to development
> within ecological limits.**

Wheeler and Shimahara ask that we develop an education that respects the interrelated "integrity" of the ecological basis for life. They have described the pre-ecological predicaments of our present society and its incompatibility with human survival. They recognize that escape from the use of science into mysticism and epistemological anarchy is not the direction we must go. Rather, they ask for a better science, combined with humanistic goals and a critical understanding of our pre-ecological culture.

But such an ecological *perspective* must be treated as a necessary but not a sufficient condition—the sufficient condition being the addition of a workable plan for transition supported by political initiative. Only integrated planning based ecological principles will permit us to escape the Malthusian law where nature does the planning through the destruction of members of the species, if we fail to plan adequately in cooperation with nature. The other side of this somber reality is that we can learn not only to survive but also to create a substantial *increase* in the quality of life, providing we transform the *meaning* of "progress."

Our thing-culture has been based on the assumption that progress would necessarily result from a gross aggregate increase in economic "goods." The word *growth* has been used ambiguously, sometimes to refer to quantitative expansion, sometimes qualitatively, as when educators refer to mental growth. When the term *growth* is put in ecological perspective we see that our economic "growth" is more analogous to biological pathology, involving *a growth* which is out of control and devouring the host. We continue to create retrogression in the name of progress.

Instead of serving our essential needs, we support the inertia and the dynamics of the old order by continuing to stress management and engineering technique. In the schools this involves the current obsession with behavioral objectives, performance criteria, and accountability procedures, without a theory which explains what behavior and performance schools ought to be held accountable for. When educators permit themselves to be merely technicians it is not surprising that they mirror the society and concentrate on know-how to the exclusion of know-what. They can then teach the "new" social studies by the use of "inquiry" method without a contextual theory of what needs to be inquired into or what needs to be done in addition to inquiring. Similarly, new math is compartmentalized and separated from the social and natural sciences and the pressing problems of society, producing analytic logic games that reward the student who plays without asking if the game is necessary or what it is used for. Vocational education becomes preparation for the best-paying job, within one's social class, whether or not the job exploits people or the environment. Physical education encourages high technology games such as bowling, status games such as golf, or competitive/aggressive team games to prepare for real life in the old order.

Individual freedom to do what one wants when one wants permeates much of the school ideology, adding another value directive—anarchy—to the supermarket called American education. With virtually no perspective on human life, planet earth, or this period of history, American education goes off in all directions intent on showing that it is impartial, neutral, fair, and therefore scientific. "Freedom" is considered American and democratic, and it takes priority to *community* and a life-affirming environmental ethic.

If ecology is understood both as an empirical science and as a metaphor, our entire way of perceiving, thinking, valuing, and behaving needs to become transformed so that it is more ecologically rooted than mechanistically rooted. If "*everything is connected to everything else,*" as Commoner points out, we need to learn to respect the organic interconnections of interdependent *social and biological systems.* The term *system* is usually used only to refer to a mechanistic metaphor instead of an organismic metaphor. Not that we should ignore mechanistic systems—we must use them—but we must use them only when they are compatible with ecological life-support systems. In American society, technosystems are religious shrines.

The combination of engineering principles and a passionate faith in engineering solutions has created what can be called *technofanaticism,* the belief that all problems have technical solutions and that anything that is technically possible ought to be done. This religion permeates all aspects of our culture. Farmers are aided by the friendly petrochemical corporations to saturate their lands with nonorganic nitrates and their crops with pesticides. The nitrates pollute the water and interfere with the nitrogen-fixing capacity of soil bacteria, and the pesticides apply chemical overkill to insects classified both as "friends" and as "enemies." The engineering metaphor is even more obviously used by the military, as we use technology to kill "enemies" rather than use politics to create cooperative interdependence. The medical profession applies broad-spectrum antibiotics with the same tactical-efficiency outlook to kill the internal "enemy," while in fact friends and enemies are equally destroyed by overkill, and the internal ecology of the body is scrambled.

Widespread dependence on drugs is part of the same outlook. Thus we have chemical engineering of altered states of consciousness in which even the human mind is manipulated by engineering science. (The gene is next on the agenda.) Once reality is perceived in fragments which are moved or controlled by the linear force of external chemical and physical pressure, the development of biological and even social community is precluded. We create reality through the metaphor by which we perceive reality, and the Western metaphor of engineering-and-the-machine continues to dominate formal and informal education.

Because technofanaticism supports the view that if something is technically possible it ought to be done, a principle of social priority is created. The war system flourishes while the peace system is moribund. The National Aeronautics and Space Administration receives billions while poverty and unemployment flourish. Detroit plans to save us with a less polluting but less efficient rotary engine, while the last few decades of the world's petroleum is devoured in a flash of historical time to serve those who need it least.

Engineering principles do not readily mix with ecological principles; one must supersede. For the Army Corps of Engineers and the Atomic Energy Commission the choice has been easy. Nature is made to be controlled, managed, and exploited. Biology had better accept orders from physics, and nature had better move over while the technician takes command.

But what other world is there, and how might we get there? *Community* rather than *organization* might be one of the keys. In a biological community the members establish their own interdependent equilibrium, in which control is shared among the members. Each depends on the other to form a cooperative survival system in which the whole is more than the sum of its parts.

An ecological perspective involves not only an understanding of the general principles of small biological communities but also understanding of macro-ecology, how the global ecosystem works, insofar as we understand it. Harmony between organisms and their environment requires a similar harmony between its individual biological members. Within nonhuman communities this "social ecology" is established largely by genetic determinants. Human societies must learn to create the requisite equilibrium in order to have community. The process must include enough cooperation and interdependence to provide shared learning and self-corrective adaptations. "Adaptation" in ecological terms cannot be merely adaptation by single members of a species; it must be species adaptation. An economic system of the kind used in the United States is pre-ecological. It involves competition, technofanaticism, self-interest, and profit making which encourages exploitation of people and nature and results in social fragmentation rather than community. Even American foreign policy emphasizes the wrong kind of stability— the retention of the status quo, the very process which encourages exploitation of nature and of other persons. Social and biological ecology require a system based on functional interdependence. The politics of the old order precludes cooperative stability and necessitates domination and exploitation. So an ecological perspective is a precondition for both revolution and survival.

Students need to learn to design a society which works in cooperation with nature, but at the same time increases rather than sacrifices social justice. The poor must not be exploited to subsidize environmental quality. It is immoral—and also bad politics. The cooperative design of an ecologically based society may itself help create community. Joint participation in the planning of the future may be one of the best ways to produce social and biological cooperation simultaneously. To enforce environmental standards by increasing unemployment ensures a crippling political reaction to environmental legislation. Environmental planning requires the guarantee of jobs which are environmentally responsible so that work is transformed rather than eliminated. Integrated social/environmental participatory planning needs to be a central political objective and a central educational objective.

"Steady state" is a term describing a society in ecological equilibrium. We are more familiar with essentially the same principle, homeostatic balance. Our bodies perspire as soon as body temperature rises, so that evaporation will cool the body until the temperature returns to the critical level which supports our life, and then perspiration ceases.

Economic systems must produce a stabilized balance between impact on the environment and the capacity of the biosphere to handle the impact without environmental deterioration; otherwise the future becomes a progressive reduction in the quality of life with eventual widespread death and human misery resulting from collapse of ecosystems. Complete equilibrium does not have to be achieved in each area of the world, but it must be achieved worldwide. Currently the negative environmental impact occurs primarily in developed nations, because of the use of the wrong type of technology and because of overconsumption. Population itself is not the direct threat; it is what people do that constitutes the threat. However, the more people there are doing the wrong thing, the more destruction there is. Currently, China's 800 million people are far less destructive to the environment that 200 million Americans. However, if the Chinese were to develop the pre-ecological industrial habits of Americans they would create four times the negative environmental impact.

A steady state world can be Malthusian or post-Malthusian. If a steady state world is not planned, the disequilibrium will produce collapse that will then stabilize into a new equilibrium. Nature always wins. Steady state systems are planned or imposed. Preagricultural societies had a steady state system held in equilibrium by the limited plants and animals that nature provided. To overhunt meant starvation. Disease also provided checks on overpopulation.

A planned steady state world can be static or dynamic. If it is static it will retain the poverty and social injustice of the present world, and life will tend to be static, always the same. But a dynamic steady state system is one which meets the requirements of ecological equilibrium while also concentrating on increasing social justice and the quality of experience. The distribution of finite resources permits a material quality of life at whatever level world population permits. The higher the population, the lower the material standard of living.

Our current pre-ecological society has not yet learned to provide dynamic qualitative development within the constraints of ecological balance. Therefore it is threatened by the concept of a steady state system. Our society has been based on the assumption that the exploitation of nature and the quantitative expansion of the economy would provide a qualitative residue. This myth is being exploded as the open, expansive thing-economy clashes with the closed, finite global ecosphere. However, people trained to pre-ecological habits often persist with a technofanatic faith in their ability to triumph over nature, and so the first signs of an energy shortage have produced a heightened determination to exploit remaining petroleum reserves more rapidly.

A central mandate for education is to teach students to design the transition to an ecologically stabilized and yet qualitatively dynamic society. This requires identifying needed changes in lifestyle, public policy, institutional goals, and therefore "human nature." They should be serving world interest rather than special interest group politics, for survival is a prerequisite to all other human goals. But we need not merely the negative goal of survival but also the positive goal of a more meaningful future that justifies optimism. We must distinguish between causality and determinism, recognizing that a variety of futures is possible and that change will be created either (1) by designing the future or (2) by permitting trends to realize themselves. The first course is the politics of optimism, the second the politics of pessimism.

Design involves tradeoffs. SSTs, half-empty jets, the ecological devastation of the war system, the use of rivers and the air as free garbage dumps, single passengers in 300 horsepower cars, air conditioners instead of fans and open windows, overheated buildings in winter, and many other signs of contemporary "progress" must be traded for more attention to social justice, meaningful work, the quality of interpersonal relationships, aesthetic experience, and recreational activities and creative arts. The economy will need to become largely a service economy (labor intensive) rather than a goods economy (capital intensive). Education and health services could expand three or four-fold. Such planning should protect future generations from the veto power of exploitative planning through recycling and conservation of nonrenewable resources.

So education, instead of diminishing in importance as it now has, must become a central factor in creating the transition, for teaching and learning are a central part of a dynamic service economy.

A major obstacle to change, especially in the United States, is that individualism has become such a central creed that there may not be the right balance between transformation of lifestyle and public policy.

An ecological perspective requires not only an understanding of the way ecosystems work, it also requires understanding of political systems and how some are compatible with ecological planning while others are not. The best illustration of the political problem was given in an ecological parable popularized by Garrett Harden and titled "The Tragedy of the Commons." It recalls a community in early England where each member of a small group of farmers grazed a cow on the small common pasture. One farmer decided to increase his profit by adding another cow, and the other farmers were no less capable of maximizing their own advantage. Soon there were too many cows for the size of the pasture. It was overgrazed. Most of the cows died and there was starvation and death in the village.

The parable is generalizable to our finite life-support system. Ecologically "this land is your land, this land is my land," but politically it is *not* held in common. Ownership of land and other nonrenewable resources is individual, corporate, or national. The earth has no system for the *common* control of the common life-support system which constitutes our common heritage. So the current political structure permits and even requires *unilateral* control, self-interest, and exploitation of the very resources on which our *common* lives depend. This fragmentation of power is what has often been called "freedom" in Western society. But freedom to do what we want to do for our own self-interest can assure that we defeat both self-interest and common interest. Unless there is a common political system for managing the "commons" of planet earth, the tragedy of the parable seems certain to play itself out. The meaning of freedom needs to be transformed from what an individual, a corporation, or a nation wants to do to serve its self-interest, to the freedom to participate in a formalized community of humankind developing common survival policy for planet earth.

A global system of control permits tyranny if it lacks representative power. (The current development of multi-national corporations poses similar dangers.) So the real choice is not between current world anarchy and a global system of resource management, for only the latter offers a basis for survival. The impending choice is between a *just* system of resource management and an unjust one. Democracy (multilateralism) has taken on an exponential increase in value, and education has been given a new mandate.

Schools are now symbiotic partners of a pre-ecological society. An ecological perspective would obligate all institutions, including the schools, to aid in the transformation. Schools should help students:

1. *Develop an environmental awareness.* See the interdependent connection between their life and the ecological life-support system. Understand self-destruct systems.

2. *Learn to practice an environmental ethic.* Act responsibly toward the environment with respect to noise, pollution, reproduction, energy consumption, conservation, recycling.

3. *Understand the limits of individual responsibility and the need for collective action.* The tragedy of the commons problem, which requires equal applications of law.

4. *Understand the characteristics of a global steady state system.* Macro-ecological criteria must guide socio-economic planning.

5. *Distinguish between a static and a dynamic steady state system.* Plan increases in quality of life rather than quantity of production and consumption.

6. *Design futures based on integrated ecological and social planning.* Increase social justice, design new forms of work,

and develop participatory planning. Make exploited minorities beneficiaries of environmental change.

7. *Identify public policy transition steps toward a just, dynamic, steady state system.* Propose the kind of legislation needed to effect the transition nationally and globally.

8. *Participate in the political action necessary to help effect new policy.* Connect theory and practice; revise both in the light of new experience; learn ecological citizenship education.

Chapter Nine

Environmental Rights:
Legal Standing
for Future Generations

We now steal non-renewables
from the rightful heritage of future generations
because they have no recognized human rights.

Human rights are a recent historical development. Under political autocracy, a special class of rights was reserved for kings and nobility, often rationalized as from "divine" origin. The idea of government by "consent" was proposed by Locke in the Seventeenth Century as a "natural right." But the experience of the French and American revolutions extended the meaning of rights to include protection from the tyranny of government, which has been the dominant American use. The legal application of rights to the American "bill of rights" in the national Constitution permitted American citizens to have some enforcement of what would otherwise have been merely a moralistic pronouncement of "rights."

The "bill of rights" places restrictions on the action of government, limiting the power of government to interfere with individual freedom in such areas as "free speech," "free press," "freedom of religion," etc. These rights were essentially "negative," prescribing what government should *not* do. Positive rights were prescribed in 1948 after

World War II through the Universal Declaration of Human Rights. This epochal shift created the idea of rights as *entitlements*. Instead of "freedom from," the other side "freedom to" was added. Positive rights included the traditional protection rights but added economic rights, such as employment and housing entitlements. Medical rights and educational rights were part of the new emphasis, based on the obligations of government. The Declaration was supported by all nations as ethical obligations of government but lacked the means to convert these obligations into enforceable law.

In subsequent years there have been new covenants and international agreements extending the positive rights proclaimed in 1948 to include support of cultural diversity, development rights for poor countries, and equal rights for women and minorities. The most glaring omissions were that: (1) No *universal enforcement structure was created* and (2) *no principles of ecological sustainability were included.*

The Stockholm Declaration of 1972 recognized the relationship between environment and basic rights, even the right to life itself. The U.N. Environmental Programme was established and driven by the Declaration. Further recognition of the inextricable connection between quality of life and ecology was made in 1987 by the U.N. World Commission on Environmental and Development. The three leading principles are:

1. All human beings have the fundamental right to an environment adequate for their health and well-being.

2. States shall conserve and use the environment and natural resources for the benefit of present and *future generations.*

3. States shall maintain ecosystems and ecological processes essential for the functioning of the biosphere, shall preserve biological diversity, and shall observe the principle of optimum sustainable yield in the use of living natural resources and ecosystems.

The trust imposed on each generation to conserve basic natural resources was given recognition in formal documents only in these last few years. There are two minimum principles proposed: (1) *Protect public health*, and (2) *Do not steal from future generations.* Current economic systems would be substantially transformed if these principles were put into enforced law. We now threaten the health of all people with economic practices that put profit above public health, and we steal from future generations by consuming nonrenewable resources, leaving pollution such as radioactivity as a permanent cancer legacy, and we continue adding debt.

"Stealing" can only have meaning if future generations have an ownership "right." During the 1970s when the Law of the Seas conferences were trying to plan for claims on ocean resources, the principle of a "common heritage" received recognition as a type of "property" right. The distinction is yet to be made in law between what might be called "use" rights as distinguished from "consumption and ownership" rights. The consumption of nonrenewables steals from future generations. For instance, a farmer who puts in his labor to obtain a wheat crop from his land should be given absolute ownership rights to his crop, which is renewable, and to sell it at the best price he can get. But if he has absolute ownership rights over the topsoil of his land, he could farm in such a manner that topsoil, a virtually nonrenewable resource, would be lost, depriving future generations of food. This category of finite, nonrenewable resources is generically the "common heritage" category. It transcends national boundaries as a right. To be enforceable, planetary rights must be part of international, national, and local law. We now must find ways to combine ethics and enforceability. New policies and new institutions are required.

The Dawn of Environmental Policy

National policies in the United States were put in late in the 1960s to require environmental impact studies for certain types of development. Standards began to develop in the 1970s with respect to air and water quality, and the most important environmental legislation in the United States was for the protection of endangered species. Protection of the spotted owl has restricted large forested areas from logging because the owl and other "indicator" species are like the canary in the coal mine which can give warning of ecological degradation. What is needed worldwide is ecological sustainability. Then species will be protected and so will future generations' claim on sustainable natural systems. When protection of the environment is dependent on market economics, all the rewards favor liquidation rather than sustainability of resources. Old-growth forests provide rapid wealth to those who cut them down. But if ecological sustainability is mandated politically, resources from forests can be extracted up to the rate they are produced, if extraction methods are used which keep the basic ecosystems intact. Many values come from forests, and resource extraction often nullifies other uses that are even more valuable. Sport and commercial anadromous fisheries depend on the quality of streams and spawning grounds, which is often degraded by logging. Water quality and rainfall levels are also affected by degraded forests. An economy based on economic benefits to individuals and corporations easily overlooks the costs to society now and in the future. The emerging new economics requires that costs that have been "externalized" and thus subsidized by the larger public, for example, resource depletion and pollution, be "internalized" as costs to the producer. Such internalization makes many standard forms of production too costly, but production costs may drive production which increases the total efficiency and permit absorption of all external costs. Ultimately, externalized public pollution clean-up and resource exhaustion produces the highest total costs, most of which are transferred to future generations.

Principles of ecological economics include the following:

1. Internalization of costs of avoiding resource depletion and pollution.

2. Movement as far as possible toward total recycling (which would reduce the need for continued mining of nonrenewables).

3. Restriction of development to levels within planetary carrying capacity (sustainable development).

The other part of new economics gives human needs first priority over personal wants and extends human rights to include environmental rights.

Beyond Constituency Politics

Established rules of what has been called democratic government are based on constituencies that predetermine that the future will be discounted and future generations will be exploited. Constituencies with varying levels of economic and political power produce the demands made on governments and the pie is divided accordingly. Any constituency without power loses out. This is obvious with the poor and the less capable. But future generations are never present, and no penalty results from their exploitation. Pollution, resource depletion, and debt are conveniently passed on. Fly now, let future generations pay later. This is the effect of "constituency democracy." Constituency politics, in the name of democracy, has no overriding ecological or ethical goals. Enforced ecological sustainability is needed, tied to *political and legal standing for future generations*. Then all rights available now are available to future generations. Anything less constitutes structural obsolescence and generational exploitation.

The Oregon Plan as Exhibit A

In 1993 we initiated a campaign in the state of Oregon to use the ballot initiative (direct democracy) as a way of placing environmental rights in the Oregon Constitution. Organizational and financial problems prevented obtaining enough signatures to get on the 1994 state ballot, but the plan is still alive for future use in Oregon and elsewhere. It incorporates the principles just described. The first text was:

1. No state action shall infringe on the right of the people to a workplace and environment protected from pollutants harmful to human health.

2. No state action shall infringe on the right of current and future generations to the benefits of sustainable natural ecosystems, free from significant impairment.

In order to provide self-executing law that is useable in courts which puts the burden of proof on the polluter and provides standing for future generations, new language was created in 1996.

The following is a draft currently receiving review. It may become the most enforceable environmental rights law, designed mainly for initial application in states' constitutions, later in the federal constitution.

Right to a Healthful and Ecologically Sustainable Environment

The people of Oregon, including future generations of Oregonians, have a fundamental and inalienable right to a healthful and ecologically sustainable environment. In order to protect and guarantee this right, the people declare the following:

(1) All three branches of government in Oregon—the executive, judicial, and legislative—have a mandatory duty to act as the public trustees and guarantors of this right of the people.

(2) In their capacity as such public trustees and guarantors, the three branches of government in Oregon are hereby prohibited from issuing any order, permit license, or regulation, or passing any legislation that authorizes an activity the pursuance of which infringes on the fundamental right guaranteed in this section to the people of Oregon.

(3) Notwithstanding any other provision of law, if the state and/or its political subdivisions fail to diligently protect this aforementioned right, any person may bring suit to stop violations of this right and to provide for adequate corrective action, including all legal remedies. Any person may bring such suit not only on his or her own behalf but also on behalf of the legitimate interests of future generations.

(4) In any suit brought by a person to enforce the aforementioned right, the burden of proof shall be placed upon the party accused of its violation to show compliance with the provisions of this section.

(5) In the event of conviction for violation(s) of the aforementioned right, a judge or jury may impose such injunctive relief and/or financial penalties, including punitive damages, as may be deemed appropriate against the violator.

(6) In the event that punitive damages are awarded, all such monies shall be deposited in a Department of Environmental Quality Education Fund, to be used for production and distribution of educational resources about this right to a healthful and ecologically sustainable environment.

(7) In any suit brought to enforce the aforementioned right, the losing party shall bear all reasonable fees and costs of litigation. For the purpose of this section, the term "healthful and ecologically sustainable environment" is to be defined as follows: (A) A healthful environment—an environment which is free from human-made harmful pollutants to the maximum feasible extent, as determined by the best available science. (B) An ecologically sustainable environment—an environment in which natural ecosystems are allowed to function in a sustainable way without significant degradation by human activities. This section is self-executing and supersedes all inconsistent provisions. This section shall become effective (month/day/year). If any part of this section or its application to any person or circumstance is held to be invalid for any reason, then the remaining parts or applications to any persons or circumstances shall not be affected but shall remain in force and effect.

The state of Hawaii had a constitutional convention in 1979 and I was involved in helping develop environmental rights language, as follows:

For the benefit of present and future generations, the State and its political subdivisions shall conserve and protect Hawaii's natural beauty and all natural resources, including land, water, air, minerals and energy sources, and shall promote the development and utilization of these resources in a manner consistent wit their conservation and in furtherance of the self-sufficiency of the State.

All public natural resources are held in trust by the State for the benefit of the people.

Each person has the right to a clean and healthful environment, as defined by laws relating to environmental quality, including control of pollution and conservation, protection and enhancement of natural resources. Any person may enforce this right against any party, public or private, through appropriate legal proceedings, subject to reasonable limitations and regulations as provided by law.

The state of Montana included similar language as the result of a constitutional convention:

All people...have the right to a clean and healthful environment. The state and each person shall maintain and improve a clean and healthful environment in Montana for present and future generations. The legislature shall provide for the administration and enforcement of this duty, (and) shall provide adequate remedies for the protection of the environmental life-support system from degradation and provide adequate remedies to prevent unreasonable depletion and degradation of natural resources.

Brazil, Costa Rica, and The Philippines have added similar language to their constitutions, an opportunity more easily accomplished when new constitutions are established. Implementation may require translation into statutory law. The usual language of a "clean and healthful environment" is very difficult for a judge or an agency to implement. How clean? Pollution is always present. How healthful? Instead the Oregon Plan puts the burden of proof on the prospective polluter by giving protection to people from chemicals harmful to human health. The polluter must show that *proposed pollution is not harmful to human health.* It is easier for a judge to tell agencies and legislatures what they must *not* do than to prescribe what they should *do.*

Environmental rights produce ethical priorities. People are first, profit second. Putting ethical principles into law sets an example for more structural reform. To avoid stealing from future generations requires that future generations have some ownership of nonrenewables. Distinctions between minerals, fossil fuels, and ecosystems are needed. The right to minerals means that they should be recycled for continual use. The right to fossil fuels is different—for when they burn, they disappear. But a tax on fossil fuels high enough to provide the capital investment for converting to sustainable renewable (solar-based) energy is needed. Sustained ecosystems require preservation of nonrenewable old-growth forests, genes of species, and forestry and farming practices that keep the topsoil and the elements of ecosystems intact.

Chapter Ten

Electing
the Future

*We now elect people
but we need also to elect
the goals they should follow.*

Eastern Europe in its rejection of Soviet central planning is in danger of moving out of the frying pan and into the fire. A market system replacement is likely to produce another extreme which sets the stage for new disasters. Neither model incorporates ecological sustainability, and if market principles determine distribution, inequality will increase.

Both forms of economics focus on quantitative economic growth. Neither uses ethical principles nor quality of life as goals. Therefore, an economics is needed that focuses on *qualitative* personal and social development which also sustains the bio-ecological life-support system.

The Scandinavian model shows more sensitivity to social and ecological values than the American model, yet no area of the world has developed a prototype ready for the Twenty-First Century. But Eastern European countries have the opportunity to choose a new direction, avoiding many of the errors of the West.

The new model should transcend the endemic obsolescence of most of the "advanced" nations. Western nations rely on pre-ecological economics which treat "growth" as synonymous with "development." Development should be individual, social, cultural, technological, and economic, but this requires common quality-of-life goals in order to have indicators which show whether change is good or bad. Western economics is tied to expansion in the name of progress, ignoring the rights of future generations to the use of irreplaceable world resources. Benefits occur now, costs are paid later by the unborn who are not here to object (a prime example of structural violence).

Pollution in Sovietized Eastern Europe is among the highest in the worlds. The government in Hungary attributes one in every 17 deaths to pollution. In the West, "free enterprise" has often been free to pollute the public. Pollution is a form of slavery in which the public loses freedom to such basic conditions of life as clean air and water in order for producers to be free to make profits but not be responsible for the consequences. Total public costs of air and water pollution is far more expensive than preventing it in the first place, making pre-ecological economics inefficient in relation to quality-of-life goals.

Solutions: New Human Rights

To have both production and a clean and healthful environment requires first that public rights to a clean and healthful environment be constitutionally based. Secondly, the costs of environmentally safe production should be born by the producer, so that pollution is not subsidized involuntarily by the public. And third, the costs of production may be passed on to the consumer in the price of the commodity. This arrangement permits a free enterprise system to pursue profit without violating basic human rights. Needless to say, the countries that are most interested in selling the ideology of market economics have not been examples of this kind of environmental leadership.

Socially controlled market economics is currently being advocated in the state of Oregon. Called the *Oregon Plan,* it will permit the public to participate in designing goals that will give direction and accountability to state government and the economics of the state.

Under this proposal, the public through a statewide Initiative will vote on two questions: (1) whether long-range planning should be mandated by the State Constitution, and (2) whether there should be public participation in the formation of alternative plans and selection of a preferred plan.

Proposed plans will be policy plans which include ethical principles based on "the worth and dignity of all people." This permits *substantive* democracy instead of only *procedural* democracy. Examples of substantive ethics-based policy include:

1. Rights of future generations to the continual use of the common heritage of nonrenewable resources.

2. Right to collectively define common quality-of-life goals.

3. Rights to a clean and healthful environment.

4. Rights to an education.

5. The right of local communities to control growth and density.

Whereas these five goals can be applied to a state such as Oregon, which is a subunit of a national system, other rights require national application. These include rights to:

1. Employment.

2. A living wage.

3. Medical care.

4. Housing.

A subunit such as the state of Oregon would be bankrupt if the above provisions were unilaterally guaranteed, for immigration from other states would swamp the state. However, democratic election of goals at the national level can be used to achieve such objectives.

The Oregon Plan represents an approach that could have application nationally and even globally. It recognizes that what is currently called "democracy" focuses political energy on elections, fundraising, media images, and election of people instead of social goals.

When "democracy" elects people but not goals, the real goals are based on the rewards for those who are elected, meaning retention of power. This is usually achieved by combining deception with media images and avoiding real issues.

The Democracy II of the Oregon Plan substitutes integrated, long-range goals for current *ad hoc* , fragmented, piecemeal, crisis management politics. A new goals-directed politics draws people into basic considerations of what they really want from the future, within the limits of what is possible. Legislators and executives can then be held accountable to public *goals* which have been *elected*.

New Economics With New Indicators

Established GNP indicators ignore the external costs of pollution and consumption of nonrenewable resources and give a deceptive indication of progress because the actual costs are not deducted from the benefits. When costs are "internalized" instead of "external-ized," the total cost/benefit calculus, as applied to the United States, indicates retrogression even though the GNP indicates "progress." An economics of real progress requires new indicators connected to new goals.

In the short term, uncontrolled market economics applied to Eastern Europe may be an exhilarating change from overly central-ized autocratic planning. But extreme rejection of economic planning because a particular form of planning was in error lays the ground-work for new error.

Fragmentation of economic activity without directional social or economical goals produces anarchy in the name of freedom, which is likely to lead to neo-fascist measures as Twenty-First Century chaos develops.

Political planning for ecological stability and common quality-of-life goals should be combined with market economics so that the political goals are overriding. If "efficiency" and "competitiveness" are treated as ends instead means to designated social ends, a future of global ecocide, inequality, and a new system of dominance seems inevitable.

A world without planning or even commitment to sustainability is not only precarious but it produces anxiety, fear, uncertainty, and alienation, encouraging drug use and escape-fantasy as a way of life.

What is needed is a legitimate basis for hope, which now requires new world goals and world structures including representative world law. Local steps toward such basic change must precede global restructuring, and the Oregon Plan may provide a basis for considering principles on which a sustainable future can be based.

Designing the Future

Since current institutions are part of the nonsustainable past, there is now a special need to reconsider education at all levels in order to prepare people for the needed transformation. The Oregon Plan requires public participation in reconsidering the very meaning of survival and progress. If high schools and colleges enter this debate, the educational and political results could be dramatic. Participation in designing and creating the future provides a basis for an education which increases the power of people to shape their institutions and reach a new phase in social evolution. By contrast, current education is largely training to increase the efficiency of the old order, without helping students evaluate whether they are becoming part of the problem or part of the solution. And, ironically, it is done in the name of "freedom."

Polls taken in both Japan and Hawaii indicated that residents thought life was better during the growth period of the 1960s, but that life was worse as the continuing expansion of the seventies produced inflation, congestion, pollution, and uncertainty about the future.

Sustainable long-term social goals are necessary as a basis for the selection of short-term goals, something a market system is unable to do. Eastern Europe needs *more* planning than ever before, but of a very different type, and consistent with democratic processes.

New nations have urgent problems that require expedient action on one hand, but at the same time any new institutional structures quickly establish a mold that is likely to have long-term persistence. The odds are that expedience will win as a way of life, unless Constitutional meta-law is established which recognizes a new world context with new human rights, new technological possibilities, and new environmental limitations.

In this period of history, people need to understand that what they do or fail to do controls the future of the planet and all its forms of life. Humans are essentially history creators. They can plan the future or merely let it happen because they fail to re-evaluate the myths that keep the old order intact.

The Oregon Plan is one example of how people can participate in decision making which gives them greater control over the future. This and other examples of *"perestroika"* are urgently needed to permit democracy and human rights to go beyond the usual fragmenting, Band-Aid process ascribed to "democracy." Equally it avoids the old belief that electing people who you trust is an adequate way to develop societal goals. We now need people we can trust who can implement societal goals.

We live in a goal-less world out of control of its inhabitants, where competition between unequals and concentrations of power by oligarchies fill the vacuum. Expanding technology moves mainly to where the power lies. Market systems respond to people's *wants,* according to their capacity to pay, whereas a humane economic system puts *needs* first. Fulfilling human needs and providing a basis for an optimistic future requires goals toward that end. Mere pluralism is not an adequate basis for coming to terms with questions of human rights and planetary management. If we continue to only be spectators of nuclear proliferation, global pollution, destruction of the life-support system, and concentrations of wealth and power, we will lose the opportunity to move toward a better world.

Democratic power now needs to be used to give direction to human civilization so that the quality of life continually increases. If laissez-faire market economics is dominant, the tail will wag the dog and the future will be dismal. But a sustainable ethics-based economics can correct the errors of current economics.

Introduction
to Section Two

Critiques of Education

"Are Children Born Unequal" had remarkable impact as a lead education article in *Saturday Review*. It was the right article at the right time and was reprinted in many education and psychology texts, used in a variety of community programs, and also translated into foreign languages transmitted worldwide by the U.S. Office of Information.

While civil rights movements were giving minorities, especially blacks, greater access to politics, education, and jobs, there were a number of "scientific" articles which tried to convince the public that poverty was the result of natural intellectual inferiority.

The article, which I co-authored with Paul Walsh, provided a powerful challenge to that belief, yet we were concerned about the implications of Cyril Burt's research on twins which claimed there were links between genes and intelligence. Burt was the intellectual guru of British education and his years of trying to "prove" that poverty was due to inferior intelligence of the working class was exactly what ruling class capitalists wanted to hear in England. Then the class structure in England could be considered "natural" and would absolve the political system of responsibility for economic inequality. Burt's "science" inhibited reform in politics and education. The rich owed him a great deal.

Arthur Jensen, a Stanford psychologist, became the American

counterpart of Burt and provided consolation to educators who wanted to believe that some students, especially blacks, were genetically inferior. Some educators therefore shifted to the "superior" student and reduced their responsibility to teach the "inferior" student.

But a bombshell broke with the investigations of Princeton psychologist Leon Kamin who found that Burt's research was faked so the conclusions would fit his ideology. In fact, two co-authors of Burt's studies didn't even exist. When the British *Sunday Times* exposed the Sir Cyril Burt fraud, the British class system lost much of its legitimacy. It had been based on social Darwinism and the belief in natural superiority. However, poverty and racism in America was usually supported by the same rationalization.

So our article came out smelling like roses with Burt's twin studies in disrepute, and it is again offered here (as the first chapter in this section) as a basis for why as educators we need to change beliefs about the potentiality of students. We need to help people see how institutional structures, especially corporate capitalism, produce a social class system that provides different educational experiences for the rich and the poor.

Two of the articles in this section discuss how economics classes make sure that students learn only capitalistic economics. We exclude economic alternatives in a country that claims to emphasize "choice." Fundamental to American educational philosophy is whether democracy or capitalism is the best model and to recognize that they are *not* the same.

Chapter Eleven

Are Children Born Unequal?

Co-Authored with Paul Walsh

> *Belief in genetic intellectual inequality*
> *has been a way of keeping the class structure intact*
> *and using education to foster discrimination*
> *against minorities and the poor.*

In societies where power and privilege are not equally distributed, it has always been consoling to those with favored positions to assume that nature has caused the disparity. When man himself creates unequal opportunity, he can be obliged or even forced to change his social system. But if nature creates inequality, man need only bow to supreme forces beyond his control, and the less fortunate must resign themselves to their inevitable disadvantage.

The metaphysics of natural inequality has served aristocracies well. The Greeks had wealth and leisure as a result of the labor of slaves. Plato expressed the wisdom of the established order with the claim that nature produces a hierarchy of superiority in which philosophers, such as himself, emerge at the top. Aristotle's belief that all men possess a rational faculty had more heretical potential, but it was not difficult to believe that some men are more rational than others.

In later periods, nations that possessed economic superiority explained their advantages on the basis of innate superiority. Sir

Francis Galton was convinced that the English were superior and that the propertied classes were even more superior than the general population. They were the repository of what was the most biologically precious in mankind.

The democracies of the new world shattered many elements of the old order, and brought a new, radical, equalitarian outlook. In principle, if not always in practice, man became equal before the law, and the idea of "the worth of the individual" established a principle of moral equality. Yet legal and moral equalitarianism did not necessarily mean that men were intellectually equal. So the assumption upon which American schools and the American marketplace developed was that democracy should mean *equal opportunity for competition among people who are genetically unequal.* This creed has satisfied the requirements of modern wisdom even for the more liberal founding fathers such as Thomas Jefferson, and it equally fit into the social Darwinism of an emerging industrial society.

In contemporary American education many of these assumptions remain. People are usually assumed to be not only different in appearance, but also innately unequal in intellectual capacity and therefore unequal in capacity to learn. The contemporary creed urges that schools do all they can to develop *individual* capacities, but it is usually assumed that such capacities vary among individuals. Ability grouping is standard practice and begins in the earliest grades. Intelligence tests and the burgeoning armory of psychometric techniques increasingly facilitate ability tracking, and therefore the potentially prosperous American can usually be identified at an early age. If it is true that people have inherently unequal capacities to learn, the American educational system is built on theoretical bedrock, and it helps construct a social order based on natural superiority. But if people actually have inherently equal capacities, the system is grounded in quicksand and reinforces a system of arbitrary privilege.

Four types of evidence are typically offered to prove that people are innately different in their capacity to learn. The first is self-evidential, the second is observational, the third is logical-theoretical, and the fourth is statistical.

The self-evidential position is based on high levels of certainty which include a strong belief in the obviousness of a conclusion. Many people are very certain that there is an innate difference between people in intellectual capacity. However, such tenacity of feeling is not itself a sufficient basis for evidence, for it offers no method of cross-verification. The mere certainty of a point of view regarding the nature of intelligence must be discounted as an adequate basis for verification.

The observation of individual differences in learning capacity cannot be dismissed as a basis for evidence; useful information for hypotheses requiring further verification can be obtained in this way. For instance, parents may notice different rates of learning among their children. People from different social classes learn and perform at different levels. The city child may learn particular skills more rapidly than the rural child. Observations require some care if they are to produce reliable evidence, but it is possible to observe carefully, and such observation can be cross-verified by other careful observers.

But if people learn particular tasks at different rates, does it follow that people must therefore be *innately* different in their learning capacity? If does *not* necessarily follow. Increasingly, as we know more about the role of environment, we see that there are not only differences between cultures, but also differences within cultures. Even within families, no child has the same environment as the others. Being born first, for instance, makes that child different; he is always the oldest sibling. A whole host of variables operates so that the environment as perceived by an individual child has elements of uniqueness (and similarity) with other children raised in proximity.

Observational evidence can be a useful part of the process of understanding when it raises questions that can be subjected to more conclusive evidence, but it is often used as a way of selectively verifying preconceived notions which are endemic in the culture. Western culture is strongly rooted in the belief in a natural intellectual hierarchy. Few observers have been taught to make observations based on assumptions of natural intellectual equality. Observational evidence must be carefully questioned, for it is often based on a metaphysic of differential capacity which encourages selective perception and *a priori* categories of explanation. Yet these preconceptions are rarely admitted as an interpretive bias of the observer.

Theories based on carefully obtained data provide a more adequate basis for reaching a defensible position on the nature-nurture controversy than either of the previous procedures. A general theory in the field of genetics of psychology which fits available information would be a relevant instrument for making a deduction about the nature of intelligence. If a logical deduction could be made from a more general theory about heredity and environment to the more specific question of innate intellectual capacity, the conclusion would be as strong as the theory. Such deduction is a commonly used procedure.

Both genetic and psychological theories have often been used to support the belief in inherited intelligence. Genetic connections between physical characteristics such as eye color, hair color, and bodily stature are now clearly established. Certain disease propensity has a genetic basis, yet the best established research is now between single genes and specific physical traits. It is commonplace to assume that if a hereditary basis for differential physical traits has been established, there is a similar connection between genes and intelligence. The conclusion, however, does *not* necessarily follow. Intelligence defined as the capacity to profit by experience or as the ability to solve problems is not a function of a single gene. Whatever the particular polygenetic basis for learning, it does not follow that intellectual capacity is variable because physical traits are variable. Current genetic theory does not provide an adequate basis for deducing a theory of abilities.

Similarly, the Darwinian theory of natural selection is often used to ascribe superiority to those in the upper strata of a hierarchical society. Yet a system of individual economic competition for survival is actually a very recent phenomenon in human history, characteristic of only a few societies, primarily in the Eighteenth, Nineteenth, and early Twentieth Centuries. It is very likely that it is irrelevant to genetic natural selection because of its recent origin. American immigration came largely from the lower classes, a fact which could condemn America to national inferiority if the Darwinian theory were used. In the long span of human history, most societies have relied mainly on cooperative systems or autocratic systems for their survival, and individual competition is an untypical example drawn largely from the unique conditions of Western, particularly American experience.

Psychological theories which emphasize individual difference have often assumed that the descriptive differences in physical characteristics, personality, and demonstrated ability are all due largely to heredity. Psychology has had strong historical roots in physiology, but as social psychologists and students of culture have provided new understanding of the role of experience, hereditarian explanation has shifted toward environmentalism. Even the chemical and anatomical characteristics of the brain are now known to be modifiable by experience. Psychologists such as Ann Anastasi point out that, "In view of available genetic knowledge, it appears improbably that social differentiation in physical traits was accompanied by differentiation with regard to genes affecting intellectual or personality development."

Anthropologists, with their awareness of the effects of culture, are the least likely to place credence in the genetic hypothesis. Claude Levi-Strauss, a social anthropologist, claims that all men have equal intellectual potentiality, and have been equal for about a million years. Whether or not this is true, it is clear that the best-supported general genetic or psychological theory does not validate the conclusion that individual intellectual capacity is innately unequal.

Statistical studies under controlled conditions, on the other hand, can provide some of the most reliable information. For instance, when animals are genetically the same, there is the possibility of inferring genetic characteristics through experimental studies. Identical twins develop from the separation of a single egg and have identical genetic inheritance. If human twins could be raised under controlled experimental conditions, much could be learned about the respective role of heredity and environment. Many studies have been made of twins, but none under sufficiently controlled experimental conditions. The results, therefore, permit only speculative conclusions. Most twins are so similar that unless they are separated they are likely to be treated alike. When they are separated, in most cases, one twin is moved to a family of the same social class as the other twin. And people of similar appearance tend to be treated similarly—a large, handsome child is not usually treated the same as a short, unattractive child. The resulting similarity of IQ scores of separate twins has not been surprising.

Even if particular identical twins were to show marked differences in ability when they live in substantially different environments, as they occasionally do, the evidence does not prove the *environmentalist* thesis unless a significantly large number of random cases is compared with a similarly random selection of nonidentical twins. In a small sample, difference could be due to the experience deprivation of one twin. It is possible to stultify any type of development, and so the variation between identical twins, identified in some studies up to forty points, by no means disproves the hereditarian position. Consequently, current studies do not provide conclusive statistical evidence to support either position over the other.

Studies of innate intelligence, then, have not produced conclusive evidence to justify the claim for an innate difference in individual intellectual capacity. Equally, there has not been conclusive evidence that the innate potential between people is equal. The research is heavily marked by the self-serving beliefs of the researchers. Psychologists have usually created "intelligence" tests which reflect their own values, predetermining that their own scores will be high. When they have discovered that they are high, they have often proclaimed such tests to be indicators of innate superiority.

Many studies are built on simple-minded assumptions about the nature of environment. Phychological environment is related to the subject. A researcher who says that two children live in the "same" environment is quite wrong, for the environment that each child perceives may be quite different from that perceived by the researcher.

Also, it is often assumed that environment is only postnatal, but evidence is now available on the role of prenatal environment, both psychologically and nutritionally. Malnutrition of a pregnant mother can, and often does, have permanent debilitating psychological and physiological effects on her child. Certain diseases contracted by the mother (measles, for example) and certain drugs (thalidomide, for instance) can produce destructive "environmental" effects which limit intellectual capacities. Clearly, people do demonstrate varying capacities to learn, but they have had varying prenatal and postnatal opportunities. If they are female, they are generally treated differently than if they are male. African Americans are too often treated different from whites—one social class is treated different from another. The *kind* of employment people engage in has a profound effect on what they become. They probably become different through different treatment and different experience, yet our institutions, reflecting our culture, usually operate on the assumption that such differences in ability are innate.

There are at least three ability models which can be supported by current evidence. Each is based on different assumptions about human nature and therefore provides a basis for different social philosophies and different conceptions of government and education.

The first model assumes a great variety of innate ability and a high level of intellectual demand on the average person. In this model, there are hereditary geniuses and idiots, while most people have an intellectual capacity about equal to the demands of their society.

The second model assumes that the innate ability potential of everyone (who has not been injured pre- or postnatally) is equal and far exceeds the normal demand level. (The actual opportunities a person has may produce differential *performance* similar to the first model.)

The third model assumes the possibility of some variation, but since all of the ability potential is well beyond the normal demand level, the variation makes virtually no operational difference.

In an economic or educational system, model Number 1 would justify the usual culling, sorting, and excluding through screening devices to create a "natural" hierarchy of ability. It would also justify the common belief in "equal opportunity for competition between unequals," where sorting is achieved through competition.

Both models two and three would justify maximum social effort to develop the abilities of all people, and the failure to achieve high levels of ability in all people would constitute social failure rather than individual failure. American society, with its considerable disparity of wealth and power, is largely a success based on the inequality assumed

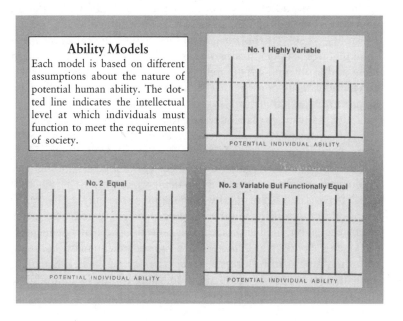

Ability Models

Each model is based on different assumptions about the nature of potential human ability. The dotted line indicates the intellectual level at which individuals must function to meet the requirements of society.

No. 1 Highly Variable

POTENTIAL INDIVIDUAL ABILITY

No. 2 Equal

POTENTIAL INDIVIDUAL ABILITY

No. 3 Variable But Functionally Equal

POTENTIAL INDIVIDUAL ABILITY

in the first of the three models. It is largely a failure based on the equality assumed in the second and third models.

Schools make little effort to develop the kind of equal ability assumed in models two and three. IQ tests are widely used to identify presumed differences in innate ability so that culling and grouping can make the management of the school easier and more efficient. The disastrous effects of the schools on lower-class children are now finally becoming known. The "compensatory" concept has gained some headway, but most educators are so overloaded with work and so traditional in outlook that the schools have become partners with the economic system in reinforcing a system of privilege that usually panders to the children of those in power and finds metaphysical excuses to make only minor gestures toward the less fortunate. The "special programs for the gifted" would be more accurately labeled "special programs for the privileged," for the gifted are primarily the children from socio-economic classes which provide the most opportunities. The less fortunate (usually lower-class children) are ordinarily neglected or convinced that they are innately inferior. Once they become convinced, the prophesy is soon realized.

Part of the problem is the way "intelligence" is defined. It can be defined in many different ways, each leading to a somewhat different educational direction. We can view it as environmental adaptation, as ability to solve problems, as ability to use logical convergent thinking, or it can emphasize divergent thinking and the creation of ideas and problems. When intelligence is defined as abstract verbal-conceptual ability drawing on the modal experiences of middle-class environment, as it is in most IQ tests, a selection has been made which excludes many other plausible and often more useful definitions.

The capacity to become intelligent does, of course, have a genetic basis. A cat is not capable of becoming a psychologist. But this does not mean that demonstrated differences in intelligence among psychologists are innate. What is particularly important is whether intelligence is defined primarily as the input or the output. The input is not subject to control, but the output depends on experience; so it is intelligence as output that should be the central concern of the educator.

Until the particular beliefs, which are endemic in many cultures, including American culture, are seen to be part of the heritage of an ancient, anachronistic, elitist tradition, there is little likelihood that the official liberal and equalitarian goals of many modern nations are likely to be realized, even though the wealth of modern technology gives every promise that they are capable of being achieved. Government, industry, education, and virtually all other institutions are now part of the problem, hobbled by a metaphysics of innate inequality. Elitist assumptions about the meaning of ability permeate all fields of education. When teachers of music, mathematics, art, or physical education find that a student doesn't demonstrate the requisite ability, they often reject him (low grades can be a form of rejection). Then counselors shuttle the student to courses where he shows "ability." All this assumes that the school should not develop abilities, but only grant them opportunity to be expressed. The Rousseauian belief in the pre-existing self is widespread.

The environmental hypothesis may be wrong, but if it is, it should be shown to be wrong only after a society has done everything possible to develop the abilities of people. We should begin with prenatal care, and should eliminate the experience of economic deprivation, ghettoized living, and elitist schools and businesses. *Lacking definitive scientific evidence about human potentialities, social policy should be based on moral considerations.* We should base our policy on the most generous and promising assumptions about human nature rather than the most niggardly and pessimistic. People will do their best only when they assume they are capable. Liberal assumptions and conservative assumptions about human nature create their own self-fulfilling prophesies. We now create millions of people who think of themselves as failures—as social rejects. Their sense of frustration and despair is a travesty on the potentialities of an affluent nation.

Poor teaching is protected in the American educational system through the assumption that the child doesn't have the ability. An American environmentalist commitment (toward liberal rather than totalitarian goals) would aim at *creating* ability, at *increasing* intelligence, at *developing* interests. The meaning of "education" would need to be broader than merely institutional schooling. It should also include community responsibility, especially for business and the mass media, which must supplement the work of the school if Americans are to receive more equal educational opportunity. This requires more social planning and more public responsibility than Americans have previously been willing to undertake.

Most American institutions, including the schools, still base their policy largely on the old conservative ideology. This outlook resists change and condemns many to inferiority. Ideological rigidity is not exclusive to the United States; in fact, many other nations are even more rigid. Yet the expanding wealth produced by modern technology is beginning to encourage the have-nots within the United States and throughout the world to demand their share by force and violence if necessary. Violence is likely to be an increasingly common road to social change unless a new public morality based on new assumptions about human potentiality is translated into both foreign and domestic policy. It is not merely racism which bogs down American progress, but also the more pervasive belief in intellectual inequality. The failure to develop the abilities of people was useful to the early American aristocracy and to the power elite of an industrial-scarcity economy. But modern economies of abundance flourish through the maximum development of the abilities of people. There is potentially plenty for all. More widespread development of the capabilities of people would not only add greatly to the wealth of nations, but it can also permit people to participate in a social and cultural renaissance.

Aside from the compelling moral obligation to create equal opportunities within nations and even between nations, the excluded millions in the world are starting to force the changes which should have occurred long ago. Some of them don't believe they are inferior, and they are understandably impatient about changing the old processes of exclusion. All institutions, including the schools, will either need to re-examine their self-consoling elitist beliefs and create real and equal opportunity, or else risk that violence and revolution will increasingly become the dominant instruments of social change.

Chapter Twelve

Have Our Schools Kept Us Free?

Intellectual conformity has been more common in American schools than critical thinking. Controversial issues have usually been avoided to protect conventional beliefs.

The most difficult goals for people to pursue are often those they claim to prize most highly. In American culture, the word *freedom* has a halo of esteem, yet the goals that Americans actually pursue are often inconsistent with the freedom they supposedly revere. Educators, themselves sensitive to cultural ideals, often praise the record of education by asserting, "Our schools have kept us free."

The statement is difficult to verify or to refute. But the assertion has such important implications that it is worth examining relevant information to see whether the evidence suggests that schools have, in fact, kept us free.

The first problem is to define the term *freedom*. Given certain definitions, one might examine any of a variety of educational outcomes and show that in some fashion each contributes to freedom as defined. If the outcomes are also desirable in a totalitarian society, they are not central in a discussion of freedom, for they do not distinguish a free society from a totalitarian society.

Freedom can be defined to include many of the elements of both a democratic (free) and an autocratic (totalitarian) education. In the recent Soviet Union, a modern autocratic political state, skills like reading, writing, and computation were intentionally developed without being inconsistent with the totalitarian ideology. Scientific information and a wide variety of technical skills were also taught. Education was free in the sense that there was no tuition, and it was universal so that all could receive it. Since these objectives are also important in a modern "free" democratic state, they are not distinguishing features of either system. What should be learned in a democratic society to free its citizens in a way that cannot be permitted in an autocratic society?

Since an autocratic society must retain an essentially closed system of ideas, thoroughly open criticism of goals and procedures is threatening to the system. Conversely, a democratic society builds its goals and procedures on the results of unrestricted critical examination. Democracy, therefore, depends on maximum criticism while autocracy considers maximum criticism intolerable. Since social criticism and the institutionalization of this process are essential features of a democratic society, though destructive to an autocratic society, *criticism may be considered the most distinguishing characteristic of a free society.* An explicit statement of these principles of freedom can provide an evaluative criterion for examining the contribution that schools make to freedom. The criteria may be stated as follows: first, individuals should understand their society and be intelligently critical of it; second, individuals should defend the institutions that are necessary to the maintenance of unrestricted social criticism.

These may not be the only criteria of education for freedom. There are others which are necessary, some of which aim at the development of individual abilities and, therefore, free the individual from what would otherwise be personal limitations. These criteria are submitted as two that are essential to education in a free society and inconsistent with education in an autocratic society. If these two criteria are among those that distinguish an education for freedom, it then becomes possible to examine the record of American education to see whether the schools have contributed significantly to these objectives. If they have not, the assertion "Our schools have kept us free" is not adequately supported.

It is not the purpose of this paper to introduce new evidence but to refer to studies that have already been conducted to see whether present evidence supports the two criteria.

The theocentric education of early America obviously made no contribution to the two criteria. The period when education might have contributed to freedom is from the mid-Nineteenth Century to the present, when the curriculum became secular and education became universal. However, since only a minority of the total population received a college education, the record below the college level is the most relevant.

Before the Twentieth Century, when the majority of students did not attend school beyond eighth grade, it is questionable that education at the elementary-school level could have made a significant contribution toward the two criteria under consideration, even if it had tried. It is evident that the elementary schools did not try, for the studies at that level were either formal or vocational, and all were noncontroversial.

During the Twentieth Century the high school has been the institution that has been able to affect the lives of nearly all Americans at a time in their development when principles of freedom could become meaningful. The American high school is therefore the institution of primary interest in this study.

Some of the most useful information on the history of freedom in the schools came from Howard Beale's studies in the 1930s, sponsored by the American Historical Society. Beale conducted the most comprehensive study of freedom in American schools that has been undertaken. The findings were published in 1941 in two volumes. One volume, called *A History of Freedom of Teaching in American Schools,*[1] covered the entire period of American education. The other volume, *Are American Teachers Free?,*[2] concentrated on the period after World War I. The following statements are from Beale's conclusions:

> Teachers in each century and locality have been allowed to discuss subjects that did not seem to matter and denied freedom on issues about which men did seriously care. (1: xiii)

> It is questionable whether the teacher of 1939 is freer to criticize the capitalist system than the teacher of 1859 was to oppose slavery. (1: 247)

Whether teachers are actually more free in matters that vitally interest the public than they have been in other days is doubtful. There seem to have been many more open violations of freedom in the past ten years than in all the rest of our history together. (1: 263-64)

The majority of teachers...are usually not aware of their own extreme conventionality. Furthermore, they have never done enough thinking or reading to know a "controversial subject" when they see one, for in their mind there can be no "controversy" or possibility of difference of opinion on any of them. (1: 247)

The average administrator opposes real freedom for teachers. (2: 744)

The study showed that there was little concern in the schools for social criticism or for the institutions that supported such criticism. Merle Curti, who conducted a historical study of the social ideas of American educators during the same period,[3] stated: "It would seem that science, religion, and philosophy were less important in determining the social thinking of educators than the pressure, however unconscious it may have been, of the dominant economic forces of the day" (589).

If such conclusions are thought to be influenced by the reformist period in which Beale and Curti were writing, studies of other leading historians of education writing more recently can be cited. In 1947, John Brubacher wrote[4]:

The rise of the public school system put a premium on keeping controversial issues out of the classroom. The success of the shift from private to public support of education depended in large part on keeping a united public opinion behind the public school. (634)

In the classroom below the college grade the problem of academic freedom was not even raised in nineteenth century America. There was no reason why it should be. The common school curriculum was so devoted to the three Rs and the academy and high school curricula were so absorbed in either classics or the practical studies necessary to getting ahead in a rapidly growing country that no one even thought of making room for a study of current social issues of a controversial nature. (633-34)

Even more recently R. Freeman Butts has stated[5]:

Social pressures upon teachers have been great. The public has been very eager to make its teachers toe the mark of respectability and conform to the dominant mores of the community. (544)

In the 1940s and 1950s the hottest issues centered upon "subversive" ideas and actions of teachers.... Several kinds of steps were taken to ensure the orthodoxy of teachers and to weed out those thought to be dangerous and disloyal.... More serious than all other aspects of these campaigns for orthodoxy was the atmosphere of fear, suspicion, timidity, and anxiety that developed in schools and colleges throughout the land. Self-appointed censors and accusers kept after teachers so energetically that few dared to discuss even the basic issues of public policy that filled the press, radio, and television. (545-46)

These historians indicate that the schools were not making significant contributions to the kind of freedoms under discussion. Other studies have provided relevant information about the recent practices of schools and the behavior of high-school students.

Late in 1955 a survey of high-school teachers was conducted throughout Arizona to determine the restrictions teachers believed existed in their teaching and in their role as citizens of the community. The findings indicated fewer restrictions than in the 1930s on the more innocuous personal activities such as drinking, smoking, and dancing. But in the freedom to teach controversial issues no improvement over the 1930s was indicated. Nearly all issues connected with sex, politics, or religion were assumed to be "dangerous." Society's more important problems were considered the least acceptable for study. The lack of freedom was attributable in part to external pressures but was based more significantly on the voluntary submission of teachers themselves. Teachers used the term "teachers' ethics" only in reference to their reason for capitulating to arbitrary social power. "Teachers' ethics" were never associated with an obligation to take action against pressures that restricted academic freedom.[6]

In 1957, Remmers' *The American Teenager* summarized a fifteen-year study by social scientists at Purdue University.[7] One of the findings was that the majority of teenage students did not believe in civil liberties. Sixty percent believed that censorship of books, newspapers, and magazines is warranted. "A third of them believed American free speech should be denied certain people if it seems convenient. Another 13 percent would restrict by law religious belief and worship" (16-17).

A recent statement by Jules Henry bears on the criteria being examined.[8] Henry, an anthropologist, has developed an outline of education based on many different cultures, including American education. Henry wrote, "Nowadays, in America, there is much talk about teaching children how to think. In five years of observation in American schools, however, we have found very little that tends in this direction" (274).

These statements are not evidence in themselves, yet they summarize findings that do constitute evidence. Possibly there is other equally creditable evidence that affirms the contribution the schools have made to American freedom. The evidence that has been cited, which seems to be representative, does not support the assertion that the schools have made significant contributions to either of the two criteria of freedom—intelligent social criticism or defense of institutions maintaining social criticism. If there is agreement on the way freedom has been defined, and if these findings are representative, it must be conceded that the assertion "Our schools have kept us free" does not correspond with available evidence. Below the college level the curriculum, teaching methods, administrative practices, and the attitudes, beliefs, and knowledge of students have provided no basis for concluding that there has been any significant concern for freedom as it has been defined here.

There may be little consolation in assuming that colleges have a substantially better record than high schools. The Jacob study suggests that the great majority of students are not more intelligently critical of their society when they graduate from colleges and universities than when they enroll; however, they do show a gain in the ability to adjust socially and to earn a living.[9]

Possibly Americans have always exaggerated their freedoms, because they have interpreted freedom largely as the absence of the tyranny of government. There are other forms of tyranny that are not always labeled as such. According to Beale, "The tendency to coerce conformity and to resort to mob violence against the dissenter from popular opinion has been much greater in American history than men have realized or like to admit" (2: 19). In recent times, as William Whyte has shown, the corporation has often sought total control over men's lives, for their behavior even in activities outside of their salaried services has been judged to reflect on the image of the corporation.[10] It appears that the statement "Our schools have kept us free" indicates only an overly generous assumption about the state of American society.

American education has surely served as a useful success ladder even if its contribution to the kind of freedom under discussion has been questionable. Merle Curti once said that our schools teach "subordination to existing institutions...inculcating the ideals of efficiency and success" (3: 586). In our quest for national purpose we need to face the question as to whether efficiency and success are presently our central goals, and if they are to decide whether such goals are likely to develop the kinds of individuals and the kind of society we really wish to have. If we actually believe in human freedom, there is no reason why our schools could not, in fact, help develop a free people. However, to make significant progress in the future will require far more energy and clarity of purpose directed toward achieving greater freedom and far less time spent proclaiming ourselves free than has been true in the past.

Notes

[1] Howard K. Beale. *A History of Freedom in American Schools*. New York: Charles Scribner's Sons, 1941.

[2] Howard K. Beale. *Are American Teachers Free?* New York: Charles Scribner's Sons, 1936.

[3] Merle Curti. *The Social Ideas of American Educators*. New York: Charles Scribner's Sons, 1935.

[4] John Brubacher. *A History of the Problems of Education*. New York: McGraw-Hills Book Company, 1947.

[5] R. Freeman Butts. *A Cultural History of Western Education*. New York: McGraw-Hill Book Company, 1955.

[6] William H. Boyer. *Conformity Implication of Certain Current Secondary Educational Theories,* pp. 180-232. Unpublished dissertation, Arizona State University, 1956.

[7] H. H. Remmers & D. H. Radler. *The American Teenager,* pp. 16-17. New York: Bobbs-Merrill Company, 1957.

[8] Jules Henry. "A Cross-Cultural Outline of Education," *Current Anthropology,* I (July, 1960), 274.

[9] Philip E. Jacob. *Changing Values in College*. New York: Harper & Brothers, 1957.

[10] William Whyte. *The Organization Man*. New York: Simon & Schuster, 1956.

Chapter Thirteen

Oversight in Value Education

> *"Values" have been given*
> *more consideration in recent years,*
> *but only as personal and interpersonal values.*
> *However, institutional values*
> *are crucial and usually ignored.*

Since it is ultimately our values that give meaning to our lives, value education has taken on the enormous task of aiding in the development of qualitative human judgment. Insofar as it has contributed to a shift from mere desire to judgments of desirability, it has added to human development. Whatever the results have been in classroom practices, it does appear that such fields as social studies have incorporated value education into much of their recent theory and instructional methodology. Value education has contributed various procedures that are, on the whole, a useful addition to theory and practice, but the techniques have not been accompanied by a sufficiently basic transformation in social theory. As a result, the dominant frame of reference for most current value education is still misguided, unwittingly a reinforcer of the status quo, and therefore largely a deterrent to basic social progress.

Most current American value education presupposes that value education should concern itself with the improvement of individual rather than collective choice. It is an agent of a political philosophy based more on social atomism than social community. We are taught to improve our choices so that we think over what it is we really want within the existing society. We are not taught to design a society that makes it possible to serve common human needs, even though one would have reason to presume this goal would have something to do with values.

The dilemma is a virtual paradigm of the liberal dilemma in American society, for though it is committed in theory to the common good, it actually provides a method largely for maximizing individual and special corporate interests, and those interests are often in conflict with the common good.

Value education usually makes use of the more objective aspects of science, such as clarity, logic, and consistency, while omitting comparative experience and any moral presuppositions that might give the slightest suggestion of "indoctrination." The result is to authorize moral neutrality as a method, and so in most value education we see little analysis of the social, economic, and political implications of even the concept of the "worth and dignity of the human person." Such value education is disconnected from the design of future institutions even though institutions and public policies are probably the dominant carriers and shapers of values.

Oversight Number One:
The Need for Moral Presuppositions

Any theory of human development must have preconceptions about the ideal toward which development should progress. And curriculum should be based, at least in part, on a theory of human development. The principle of "the worth and dignity of the human person" may sometimes become a cliché, but if its implications are applied to both interpersonal relations and institutional values (which includes public policy) it can become the major premise in value education. It requires that the teacher not only try to be responsible to aid in educating each student, no matter what race, creed, social class, sex, or personal attractiveness, but it also requires that the teacher and curriculum aim toward developing responsibility on the part of the student toward other people.

This precommitment would affect the "right" way to think about such a question as whether or not those who are dying from starvation might be considered expendable because they contribute to the "solution" to the food problem. It predetermines whether it is right to kill under conditions of war if the justification is to support one's nation or to eliminate an "enemy" that believes in the wrong ideology.

Radical moral equality would be involved in the selection of children's books, that so often support racist, sexist, or nationalist values. If "the worth and dignity of the human person" is the basic axiom, and if those books indoctrinate an exploitative set of values that violate this principle, they should not be used except as bad examples.

The moral growth of children would therefore not be "free" (which is a myth); it would be directed (as it always is). But instead of being directed toward acceptance of conventional exploitative ideologies as it now usually is, it would be directed toward concern for human life. Much American education, in its hidden and overt forms, is directed toward egocentricity and individual "freedom." It is a formula for irresponsibility and isolation, and it inhibits the development of the qualities of a responsible person and teaches the more immature goal of individual "freedom" from authority. But freedom from authority is not really freedom, for our life is always part of a context and therefore a structure. American anti-totalitarianism encourages freedom from all structure in order to escape oppressive structure. The only structure that most value education provides is the structure of intellectual analytic technique. This does not necessitate the older indoctrination of the "right moral and spiritual values" which were often narrow-minded assumptions about human nature based on ethnocentric views of human destiny. The "human person" principle is anti-ethnocentric and radically humanistic. And it has been represented in various ways in certain established traditions.

One type of "humanistic" tradition is based on the principle that knowledge should serve humanity rather than be an end in itself. Medical schools have such a "bias." They do not endlessly debate whether there is some ultimate philosophical basis for deciding whether life is good or bad before they get on with the work of curing the sick and helping people prolong their lives.

The values of the human person and the equality that it implies have been recently represented through the policy of "affirmative action," which has affected all American institutions including the schools. Racial discrimination with respect to previous employment has been counteracted through compensatory hiring. The equality principle has made it absurd to debate whether racism is right or wrong; rather it makes it necessary to conduct responsible inquiry leading to social action to correct instances of such discrimination. If the schools recognize their moral obligation, they will also move into other applications of the principle of "affirmative action," especially those that would help correct traditions in which economic and political institutions have violated basic morality by institutionalizing poverty, war, and ecocide.

Oversight Number Two:
The Need for Institutional Values

The need for improving human choice with respect to interpersonal values is obvious these days, and much of the educational literature, including the trends toward humanistic psychology, are designed to encourage responsible interpersonal relations. However, political value education bearing on the development of public policy is conspicuous by its absence. Where it is taught it usually focuses on band-aid alternatives to minor social issues rather than the design of institutions that will eliminate such major pathologies as poverty, war, and ecocide.

In addition to developing responsible individual choice *within* existing institutions, the development of choice *between* institutions should be included. Alternatives to present institutions therefore need to be illuminated, and we might identify examples, the first with respect to national sovereignty.

What are the positive values of national sovereignty? What are the negative values? Is war, including atomic, chemical, and bacteriological war, part of the price of autonomous national authority? Is national competition for resources and profit inherent in the present system? Is the dominance of strong nations one of the consequences of the nation-state system, and is the global gap between the rich and poor one of the results of national autonomy? Is the continuation of the present system sensible?

What are the alternatives and are the alternatives any "better" with respect to their effect on people and on the ecosphere? Various forms of regional federation, limited world law, and also full world law and government should be examined.

In addition to alternatives to the nation-state *system,* other basic systems alternatives need to be examined. What are the effects on poverty of different kinds of economic systems? Do some economic systems predetermine unequal distribution of income and wealth? Are there ways of designing economic systems so that they eliminate poverty? What distribution *ratio* would be feasible and morally responsible in the U.S. within 10 years? What should be the long-run goal? What is the current ratio? What steps should be taken toward achieving a more equitable American economic system? What steps should be taken worldwide?

Notice that these series of questions presuppose that poverty is bad, that it can be changed, and that its retention therefore is based on structural immorality that permits the continued exploitation of people. It therefore does not focus mainly on individual choices within the present system but on alternatives to the present system. It elevates freedom to a new level of choice involving people controlling their institutions for the common good.

The current ecocide is subject to similar value analysis. One can talk about individual responsibility for reduced energy consumption, litter, etc., or else give central consideration to economic systems change. If the economic system were planned in such a way that it was required to sustain ecological equilibrium, it would be a "steady state" economic system that delivered goods and services within the framework of what the life support system will permit without deterioration. So inquiry questions might be: At what points are economic growth and expansion destructive to necessary ecosystems? What kinds of technologies can be used to reduce environmental impact? How can we stabilize population, consumption, and production? What quality of life do we want within alternatives that are ecologically feasible? What transition steps are necessary to achieve an ecologically responsible economic system? What new laws and institutions are necessary nationally and globally?

Once again the entire concern for systems change is grounded in a concern for human life, but the concern is applied to one of the *contexts* in which those values arise . Without the context the value questions are reduced to questions of individual responsibility within existing economic systems; when the ecological context is considered, the problem becomes one of designing the appropriate transformation of the system. No significant change is likely to occur without fundamental systems change.

One system can be eliminated only by substituting another. The automobile transportation system will not be changed by *eliminating* transportation, either voluntarily or through public planning. Rather it will be transformed when other systemic alternatives are substituted. The war system cannot be eliminated until there are plans to substitute a peace system. The economic inequity system requires substitution of an equity system. The cancerous effects of an endless economic "growth" system requires the substitution of a steady state system in ecological equilibrium.

When a teacher guides students into a value analysis of some of the most important value questions, it requires study of models of integrated systems alternatives. The failure of the progressive education era and of much recent "alternative" education has been that it was vacuous, for it either encouraged individual laissez-faire hedonism, or it applied inquiry into bits and pieces of ad hoc, short-range problems, often taken from news headlines that illuminated the foam on the ocean rather than the central currents. Our present period of history requires that unless we learn to plan collectively, integratively, and systemically, we are denying the possibility of choice, freedom, and probably even survival.

We now live in a world where rational short-range goals are likely to produce unwanted long-range effects and where the self-interest of sub-groups is likely to be contradictory to the needs of the larger society. So the wrong *context* for making value judgments is likely to be counterproductive to common human race values and to the development of plans for their realization.

Oversight Number Three:
The Need for Comparative Experience

Value education is usually described as a very rational, cognitive process, in which the teacher is expected to help students think logically and to examine evidence and assumptions so that alternatives and consequences are more carefully considered. All of this is useful, but the examination of alternatives is usually restricted to intellectual judgment based on involvement in the activity being assessed, for experience expands the self and provides a basis for more empathy and identification with others which changes the context in which judgment is made.

But even involvement in new experiences is not likely to be adequate without some comparison. Comparative experience has long been advocated by those who have supported "cross cultural" experience. Whether the experience is cross cultural, cross social class, or cross vocational, the principle remains the same. We usually cannot evaluate adequately without undergoing an experience and comparing it with contrasting experience.

Stated so boldly, this premise seems unoperational. How can we undergo all experiences in order to evaluate them? Clearly, we cannot, and so we must judge similarities between experiences we have undergone and those new situations we are judging. And we must use vicarious experience in the form of art, literature, role-playing, and reports of others when direct experience is unattainable.

It is hard for overfed Americans to empathize with the increasing millions throughout the world who are now starving. Temporary fasts or periods of a week or two on reduced food intake could at least give some sense of the pains of hunger. The point is not to make people miserable unnecessarily but to provide a better sense of identification with those who are victims of mal-distribution of food and obsolete politics. If concern can be generated by such empathizing experiences, the next step is to identify ways of helping the hungry. Such plans could involve short-range goals to help the current needy and also longer range plans to develop ecological and population stabilization and equitable political-economic planning.

Polls that try to measure satisfaction often have little meaning. When people are asked to make judgments about job satisfaction, they need to have some basis for comparing alternatives. To know what other jobs are like may require not merely observation of different jobs but even some direct work experience with them. This principle is incorporated into the work experience of people in China. Professors, doctors, and managers rotate with farmers and factory workers, at least occasionally, so that each will learn from the other and so that a broader appreciation of the social value of different kinds of work and new career choices will develop. Human development is the central goal rather than economic efficiency.

Antioch College has a long-established tradition of incorporating the principle of comparative work experience. Cultural exchange of students and teachers recognizes the same need for situational comparison. Work experience programs and "schools without walls" can be arranged to encourage evaluation through comparison. Yet the value-education movement of recent times has largely ignored this principle. The refinement of intellectual technique has dominated most of the theory. It is ironical that value education has resorted so largely to technique solutions, since the obsession with technique is itself a central characteristic of the *quantitative* values on which our economic-centered society is based. Value education is presumably concerned primarily with *qualitative* judgment.

Without comparative experience, the narrow range of experience characteristic of the social roles in most societies will restrict value judgment to the meaning framework of prior experience. In an established slave society, both the masters and the slaves are likely to consider their roles as normal, and any evaluation of alternatives is likely to be hypothetical until the meaning of a change in roles becomes plausible and apparent.

Enormous amounts of political energy are likely to be released when life alternatives such as new job opportunities become possible in the minds of those who have been conditioned to accept a demeaning view of their potentialities. But evaluation of comparative desirability of different kinds of work cannot occur merely by studying job descriptions. It requires experience working with people who do such work. If the doctor's son could work with the garbage collector and the garbage collector's son could work in a doctor's office, new aspirations and appreciations could develop. The urban student could work on a farm and the farm students could work in an urban setting. Other similar forms of basic social-political-cultural-esthetic contrast needs to be part of the input of value education.

Summary and Conclusions

The dominant assumptions of the recent value-education movement are based on an ideology of individual choice within existing social-cultural-economic-political systems. Choices include appraisal of minor reform but seldom of fundamental structural transformation, even though most of our collective habits, institutions, and traditions are now rapidly becoming obsolete.

Commitment to "objectivity" and fear of "indoctrination" has resulted in throwing the baby out with the bath and has precluded precommitment to people in favor of analytic technique. Both are needed, for humanistic precommitment applied to social systems would mean a value stand against poverty and for economic justice, against the war system and for a peace system, against ecocide and for ecological equilibrium. Intellectual technique should be used to show how these values can be achieved and maximized; *schools through curriculum policy should take an explicit stand in favor of such values.* Education should help people clarify the goals and examine responsible steps for achieving such goals.

But without personal involvement in the meaning of some of the alternatives, value choice may be vacuous and empty. So value education should include a greater range of comparative experiences. Instead of career education to reinforce the present obsolete economic system, work of various kinds should be compared, to judge the intrinsic satisfactions and to explore the social use and the environmental effects of such work. Schools should help people learn to *plan public policy which would create new jobs* and recognize that since we become what we do, work shapes our values and much of the meaning of our life. So our aspirational values should be used to transform the economic system and the jobs it provides.

These proposals are offered to help shift the ideology of current value education toward a human community framework in the context of world ecological problems. They do not pretend to constitute a complete theory of value education, only an attempt to help counteract some of the oversight to which most value education currently contributes.

Chapter Fourteen

Teaching Capitalist Economics in American Public Schools

There are three kinds of economics—
socialist economics, ecological economics,
and capitalist economics.
But American students are only taught capitalist economics.

Economic education in American schools is often inadequate, and what is offered has usually been based on capitalist economics. Although there is no obligation in any constitutional oath for teachers to serve capitalist ideology, the economics of capitalism is so much a part of American life that schools rarely consider alternatives to capitalism, such as economic democracy. If they were considered, the results might be as follows:

Instead of accepting the belief that "the market" and supply and demand are laws which determine economics and the future, a whole range of political-economic choices could be considered, involving human rights and common quality of life.

The use of economic "trends" in planning would therefore

give way to the design of social goals, and planning would be given a more central role in controlling the uses of the economic system.

Distribution ratios for national wealth and income could then be changed and new tax laws and employment opportunities would serve the new distribution goals. Nonrenewable resources would be treated as human capital which should also serve future generations. The consumption of such resources to produce profit to whomever has the money to buy thereby becomes obsolete.

Students would learn the ways in which monopoly in labor, corporations, and resources ownership can and currently does become highly influential in determining production and distribution. They would learn how democratic economics could shift power into the public domain.

Instead of treating Gross National Products (GNP) as the ultimate standard of progress, the overall quality of life would become primary, and environmental planning could be used to produce a high common quality of life on a sustainable basis.

The right to socially useful employment at a living wage then becomes a major educational consideration. Rights to a livable and healthful environment are given more emphasis as economic goals.

The need is for an ethically based economics that serves the public good. Schools should not be used to serve the private interests of special interest groups at the sacrifice of the larger public interest, even though conventional economic education such as that provided by the Joint Council on Economic Education is built around such social atomism.

It is doubtful that students have a basis for being optimistic about the future from the standpoint of employment and a livable environment if conventional economic policies continue. Inflation is destroying their capacity to have housing and market-based medical costs undercut their access to medicine.

The teaching of obsolete knowledge is both dangerous and immoral, and if our young people turn to drugs and other forms of escape because the future and the present seem to be grim, we need to help them use education to go beyond the determinism of "trends." This means learning to redesign the rules of the economic game so that their own growth is part of the process of understanding and participating in the creation of a better future.

Chapter Fifteen

Economic
Miseducation

Capitalist corporations have been effective
in having the "correct" kind of economics
taught in American schools.
The result is widespread illiteracy
about non-capitalist alternatives.

Introduction

Though public education is the central institution in a democracy
for providing citizenship education, schools are constantly under
pressure to serve private-sector interests. The successful intrusion of
such interests has produced public-sponsored schools that often serve
primarily private-sector goals.

Public education in a democracy not only has to be concerned with
equality of admission to public education, but it is equally important
for students to study about common human problems once they are in
school. People in a democratic society must have an intellectual basis
for responding to social needs through public policy.

Instead educators have usually permitted public schools to be
supermarkets for special-interest groups. As with the food supermar-

ket, some products are likely to be included instead of others. The more powerful private-interest groups, dedicated to their own self-interest, are likely to win—if for no other reason than that money buys materials and programs.

If this control of education continues, there is less chance of having a government that really serves the public interest. Instead, government is likely to continue to be unable to generate the necessary *public* policy.

The following article is a case analysis of this problem, with respect to one important area of school curriculum—economic education.

The Joint Council on Economic Education

The Joint Council on Economic Education was organized in 1949; its influence over economic education in American high schools and colleges has been substantial and increasing. The Board of Trustees is a mixture of public school administrators, college professors, presidents of business corporations, and union representatives. The Council supports economic education centers throughout the United States, provides publications which give new direction to its work, and develops instructional material. These reports repeatedly urge "objectivity" and "a rational, unemotional approach" to economic education. In 1974, the Council's "objectivity" brought praise and support from AT&T, H. J. Heinz, Xerox, Rockwell International, Uniroyal, Armstrong Cork, and such a substantial number of other businesses that the list looks much like Dow Jones and Associates. Exxon has provided funds to support an economic game called "Teaching Economics in American History" which is used by centers of economic education, carrying Exxon advertising into the schools.

The latest major publication illustrating the philosophy of the Joint Council is called *A Framework for Teaching Economics: Basic Concepts* (1977). It helps reveal why American business likes this form of "objectivity." The Framework indicates that the project was sponsored by General Motors, Ford, and American Telephone and Telegraph.[1] It is not a narrow ideological tract in any sense, but it clearly plays up the importance of certain concepts and plays down the importance of others while often making revealing omissions.

A first clue to its bias is the publication's failure to admit to the inherent political or ideological nature of economic theory. Economics, which they label a "science," describes "how people use productive resources to satisfy their *wants*" (emphasis mine).[2] Economics is treated as a *descriptive* science. If it were defined as a *design* science, it might be said to deal with "how people *could* use productive resources to satisfy their *needs.*" But that change in definition would constitute a different kind of economics.

The kind of economics the Joint Council favors consists of "satisfying people's *wants* for goods and services."[3] It favors a "market economy" in which "demands emanate from *individual* choice.[4] Advertising is not mentioned as a factor influencing choice.

The *Framework for Teaching Economics* also refers to "our" economy, clearly implying an American rather than a global frame-of-reference. It is claimed that "market prices constitute the principal allocating mechanism of the American economy," in spite of the abundant evidence that monopoly and oligopoly in industry is commonplace in the United States and that "administered" prices are part of the system. The fact that American industries have repeatedly formed conglomerates, interlocking directorates, and multi-national cartels is a well-kept secret in Joint Council materials. Students are, rather, guided into the "religion of capitalism," as Schumaker calls it, by a process that few are likely to find objectionable because "reality" is described through familiar landmarks given to us for years by the daily newspaper and such objective sources as *Time, Newsweek,* and *Fortune* whose good works are sponsored by the same group of sponsor-advertisers that find the Joint Council to be such a worthy educational endeavor.

The Council's "economic goals" are, conveniently, "freedom, economic efficiency, equity, security, stability, and growth." Freedom translates narrowly to be individual choice in the marketplace. Efficiency is said to be "central to economics," while equity is "an elusive concept." It is admitted that "growth is a less universally accepted goal today than it was a decade ago,[5] but it is not explained why. The reader is told that individual self-interest is the main motivating force behind economic behavior and Adam Smith is cited as a key figure in connection with economic history while Marx is nowhere to be found in the recent Framework.

While the Joint Council neglects to discuss economic systems outside the market economy, it does provide a fairly broad base for economic education within liberal capitalism, including Keynesian concepts and going beyond classical capitalism. This kind of economic education is faithful to the dominant ideology of the American business community, the government, and the majority of the academic economists. One Council publication trying to attract business money openly states, "National economic literacy is important to business because surveys reveal an anti-business bias among college graduates...and as pointed out in a *Fortune* editorial, JCEE's program chips away at this problem through improved teaching of economics at the college level."[6]

Capitalist Ideology and American Schools

American education is vulnerable to this kind of private-sector special-interest influence because too few educators have identified the conflicts between the "democratic" goals schools claim to serve and the values of capitalism. Neither the competitive, self-interest individual of the free market nor the corporate monopolist who controls supply and prices are examples of any meaningful form of democracy, for neither laissez-faire nor autocracy are values central to democracy. In the spectrum of political ideologies, it is "democratic socialism" which is built on the principle of using democracy in both the political and economic arenas.

However, the philosophy of the Joint Council directs students toward liberal and conservative ideologies.

Some Basic Errors

Joint Council material appears to be quite an admirable attempt at broadening the level of economic literacy, but in actuality it uses the "disciplines and structure of knowledge" concept of education which takes the conventional academic principles of economics as the basis for education and excludes many of the realities of the economic decisions that are being made in the "outside" world. A tough-minded approach to economic concepts and their theoretical interrelations needs to be tied to the realities of decision-making in a society where power is often unequally distributed and where economic decisions are often a way for one group or country to exploit another. The real effects of self-interest and profit motives are often shocking, as when farmers and ranchers use pesticides and hormones up until the day of marketing and contribute not only to their profit but to the cancer rate of their customers as well. We see the same behavior when businesses lobby for expansion of the military system because arms manufacturing is such a profitable activity.

It should also be pointed out that Joint Council ideology is weak on ethical considerations (what "ought to be") and strong on ethnocentric ideologies and descriptions of the recent game plan. Therefore, when value judgments are made by students they are encouraged to accept the existing system and make ad hoc choices within it on a self-interest basis. This restricts people's capacity to change the economic game plan (system) and promotes the retention of the current power structure. It plays down or omits choices in which economics serves social needs through public democratic control of production and distribution. It particularly ignores the important fact that economic systems are prime examples of "the social construction of reality"[7] in which different *kinds* of economic systems contribute to the development of different *kinds* of people so that economic systems must be judged as *educators*.

We Become What We Do

People are strongly affected by any social process, including an economic process, with its value-loading and selective rewards . No social process can be treated as value-neutral; even economic systems shape our character and our personality and cannot be mere technique.

The experiences people undergo in economic activities are fundamental to what they become and to the kind of society that develops. Competitive economic systems don't create cooperative societies. Employment which exploits other people or destroys natural resources takes its toll in either adjusting people to immoral conditions or in giving them a sense of alienation, often producing a high price in crime, drug use, and self-destructive behavior.

If an economic system excludes democratic principles and human development goals for the sake of efficiency and profit, it becomes a game that produces products at the price of people. Unless the "worth of the human person" is an ethical meta-economic principle, people can be treated as little more than one more pawn in the game—one of the "costs" to be reduced, along with capital and land costs. The "costs" and "benefits" of alternative economic systems need to be considered in ethical terms, for an economy is a social invention and should serve people.

The kind of tacit acceptance of the "compulsory unemployment" of millions of people, especially youth, minorities, and older people should be treated as economic failure which is grounded in nonethical economics. People are miseducated into thinking there is a surplus of people looking for too few jobs in such areas as education, health, and housing construction—even though there are many unmet social needs in these areas. Students are encouraged to go into areas of "need"— such as business. But if the problem were defined as a shortage of jobs rather than a surplus of people (of teachers, for example), the design and creation of new jobs could be undertaken. This is a different approach to economics in which production follows social need rather than individual "demand" measured through spending power.

Economics and the Future

The kind of future we will have is connected with and will follow upon the kind of economic system we have, and the kind of economic system we will have in the future is affected by the kind of economic education people get today. The myth of value-neutral economics prevents the larger freedom to make choices about the common future. It prevents us from recognizing that economic decisions have ethical consequences and should be treated as applied ethics.

A redirected economics education can help people learn to plan economic transition steps toward a better life for present and future generations, a consequence unlikely through the current form of economic education.

Notes

[1] *A Framework for Teaching Economics: Basic Concepts,* W. Lee Hansen, Chairman, The Joint Council on Economic Education, 1977, p. iii.
[2] *Ibid.,* p. 7.
[3] *Ibid.,* p. 10.
[4] *Ibid.,* p. 13.
[5] *Ibid.,* p. 26.
[6] "Achieving Economic Literacy Through Education and How The Joint Council is Going About It," The Joint Council on Economic Education, 1966, pamphlet.
[7] See, Berger & Luckmann, *The Social Construction of Reality,* Anchor Books, 1967.

Introduction
to Section Three

War Prevention Education

Articles in this third section were built on my experiences in the Army Air Force in World War II, in the post war Germany democratization, in my role as an Education Advisor in the army, as a high school teacher of social studies, and in university teaching as a developer of new programs in peace studies and war prevention. My first book was on militarism, titled *Education for Annihilation.*

The articles shift from the conventional national perspective to the world perspective of how to survive in a world where nuclear weapons have made war into mutual annihilation. I developed some of the earlier university courses in world order studies for teachers, often working in cooperation with the World Order Studies program originated by Richard Falk and Saul Mendlovitz. Betty Reardon worked with many of us nation-wide to develop a "world order" curriculum that was adopted by the National Council of Social Studies. The article "World Order Education: What is It?" explains this achievement.

The "war system" is the essential concept for understanding how basic systems change is necessary to promote and assure human survival in the nuclear age.

Chapter Sixteen

Defining
Peace Studies

> **Students need to know the best theories
> on how to prevent war and how to achieve
> a more peaceful world.**

The field of peace studies must meet the general requirements of
higher education, yet have its own distinguishing characteristics.

General Requirements

Meeting academic requirements of higher education means that
theory building must be rational, evidence must be empirically
verifiable, and problem-solving models must be logical and connected
to documented reality. These requirements proscribe mystical beliefs
and ideological proselytizing, assuring that peace studies are subject
to much more stringent standards than activities and methods common in religious groups and in the "peace movement."

Peace studies, however, should be no more neutral than some
established university programs. Public health programs are ethically
biased in favor of human life and do not give equal time to proponents
of sickness. Universities do not presume that their humanities pro-

grams should be neutral and balanced with inhumanities programs. Being against human violence requires being *for* human life and dignity. The "Worth and dignity of the human person" should be an ethical assumption, which provides a basis for opposing violence against people and justifies looking for the best solutions to what should be classified as "a problem."

Though peace studies should not be neutral, they should be objective. Evidence for problems and solutions should be objectively analyzed and subject to criticism, dialogue, and cross-verification. This means peace programs are not propaganda for sentimental utopianism nor romantic escapes from the tough realities of social change. Peace programs must be as objective as the social science disciplines from which they draw heavily. They are, however, ethically goal-oriented (the social sciences ought to be, too). They must presume that conditions of social life or proposed public policies that try to justify human exploitation—such as racial superiority, national superiority, or the legitimacy of economic or political oligarchy—are anti-ethical and part of the problem.

Distinguishing Characteristics

Peace studies should focus on structural violence primarily as it occurs in the international system. Peace studies should look for remedies and solutions to international violence and exploitation, and obstacles to solutions may include ideologies, cultures, and structures of dominance. But if we define our area too broadly, to include all forms of violence and exploitation, we are likely to try to achieve too much and actually achieve too little.

The entire area of conflict resolution is too broad, particularly when it includes interpersonal conflict. The conflict caused by the nuclearization of national military power is so serious and so urgent that it constitutes a threat to the entire human race, and no other contemporary issue takes priority over the urgent need to prevent war, especially nuclear war. (Existence does precede essence.) A peace program that has other priorities than war prevention should make them explicit and should be ready to offer a rationale for such priorities. Otherwise, students and the public should normally associate peace studies with *war prevention*.

A world without war is not likely to be peaceful, but if nuclear war can be prevented, there should be time to survive and work for the many educational, economic, and political conditions that can increase social justice and human community. The presumption that better interpersonal relations will change political structures and eventually prevent all war is a romantic notion contradicted by current understanding of the systemic and structural causes of war.

Though war prevention should be our central focus, closely related issues may be considered, such as the structure of dominance in the international system and its effect on economic justice and the global ecological life support system. The problem of combating terrorism—through such means as military reprisals or by offering access to political goals through world law—is a defensible subject. Whether war is merely one form of terrorism must also be confronted.

Peace studies should include the general methods of all good programs: understanding the past, the present, where trends are leading, and the assessment of feasible and desirable alternatives. But with war as our central issue, we can open up inquiry that has often been overlooked. An historian might ask: "What could have prevented a particular war? Anticipatory diplomacy? Or was the war caused by the *lack* of law in the international system in which national military power is ultimate authority?"

Our students, unlike most college graduates, should be able to enter the public arena with a theory of war prevention that they can affirm and defend in the face of conventional arguments. They should be able to enter the peace movement and improve theory, which is largely *ad hoc*, reactive, and short-range, and lacking a vision of a future where war is far less likely.

Our students should be able to analyze conventional arguments such as these: that war is caused by human nature, that economic justice will eliminate war, and that technological systems alone—such as Star Wars—can solve complex political problems. They should understand the likely consequences of nuclear war. They should clearly grasp the nature of war: as a human invention, as a political and social institution, and as integral to the current international system.

Emphasis on Structural Causality

The concept of structural causality is critical to understanding the operation of political and social systems. Yet few people understand that human events are primarily determined by institutions and the rules connected with them. The war system is invented and identifiable, yet conventional wisdom treats war as an aberration rather than as a predictable function of an obsolete international system that makes military power the ultimate instrument of conflict resolution. Traditional diplomacy is largely a form of crisis management, of reacting to events provoked by the chaotic global system; it cannot compensate in the long run for the structural power of the war system. With the potential for human accident, miscalculation, and madness, and with computers always prone to human error, nuclear war becomes ever more probable over time.

Nearly all conventional social science, even when it is attuned to structural analysis, has used "positive" causality as its frame of reference, ascribing causality to an antecedent event either in the past or anticipated in the future. Yet it would not be possible to anticipate antecedent and precipitating events prior to war with sufficient success to give us much assurance that nuclear war could be averted. "Positive causality" with its emphasis on what is *in* the system does not provide an adequate basis for a theory of war prevention nor a peace studies program.

"Negative causality," such as the absence of world law or any structure for the nonviolent adjudication of war-producing conflict, may be our most useful analytic and problem-solving construct.

People can easily understand the practical effects of substituting law and order for anarchy. They know of the need for the court and the sheriff in the American westward migration. They are ready to abandon the belief that war is rooted in human nature when they understand why the state of Oregon and the state of California will never go to war over the border dispute that currently exists. National law is already institutionalized to adjudicate and enforce a decision if a serious conflict arises. People readily see the analogy in the international system and can bring local experience to bear on the global problem of war.

Within the university setting we have colleagues in international relations whose academic traditions have often been limited to descriptive and analytic inquiry. Because we are concerned with solutions rather than merely descriptions and comparisons, we represent a different though no less rigorous conception of the academic role. We require the problem-solving emphasis found in some futurist programs and often in public planning. The recent breed of political science faculty who operate under the label of "political design" are close to our philosophical orientation. Economists whose concern is broader than conventional market analysis are often ready to join in the important area of economic transition planning, necessary if the war system and its related military economy are to be transformed.

When our goals and objectives are clear, we can freely draw from many willing and competent people in a great variety of academic areas, including the humanities. Faculty may move in and out of peace studies programs or offer peace-related courses in their own departments, with the courses cross-listed in a peace studies program. Peace studies may or may not offer degrees and can be organized as an area of emphasis, without the need of new program authorization. We should clarify and democratize language to make issues understandable to an unspecialized public, who have the political power to change public policy.

We and our students may be personally involved in partisan politics, but our programs in higher education should be pre-political, separate from actual partisan politics. We are concerned with the intellectual tools and theory for helping students become intelligent and effective, but activism should be only in the form of internships or the study of action groups, and should not serve partisan politics for university credit. We must assure administrators in higher education that we play by the rules of academia.

Because the word "peace" is ambiguous, labels such as *Alternatives to War, War Prevention, Global Transition Studies, International Conflict Resolution,* or *World Order Studies* may be more denotative and clear. When our goals are clear, it is not difficult to have a clear label for our programs. "Peace Studies" *is usable if it doesn't promise too much and deliver too little.*

Chapter Seventeen

War Education

> **The United States has developed
> a military vision of the world,
> reflected in war production and in world politics.**

Conventional wisdom tells us that things are the way they appear to be. Institutions are merely the means to the goals they claim to serve. The military establishment is merely a means to national defense. A nation needs to defend itself, so in a militarized world we must have armed forces, and they must be the best the nation can afford.

We have built national policy on conventional wisdom. We first created a capacity to defend ourselves against attack. When ICBMs with nuclear warheads made defense impossible, we changed to a strategy of offense, and counted on a balance of terror for our defense. We worked to achieve a "balance" in our favor, and so effected a persistent escalation of terror. Finally the burgeoning armament on both sides produced the capacity for mutual annihilation. Yet the arms race continued and resulted in the era of overkill. We then gained national security through a policy based on the escalation of overkill.

A shift in political language has corresponded with the military transformation. National security has been based on containment, deterrence, and nuclear brinkmanship. Justification has been grounded in the need to defend the "free world." Such policy, based on an assumed absolute goodness of our goals, has needed no reconsideration. The effort has gone instead to research and development of an ever more advanced and powerful military technology. Conventional wisdom has assured us that reliance on technical superiority is the only sane road to national security. Unconventional wisdom would assert that it is a likely road to international annihilation.

No nation easily admits that the traditional beliefs are no longer valid. Most Americans are especially unlikely to accept basic criticism of national political-military policy, for the conventional way produced military victory for all those Americans who have survived two world wars. The dead were not victorious, but most Americans survived. So the escalation of nuclear terror has seemed wise to most surviving Americans, but certainly not for Japanese survivors of the bombing of Hiroshima.

Those who do not accept conventional wisdom question whether things are the way we assume they are. Institutions may not be doing what they claim to be doing. Means may not be merely instrumental to ends, they may *determine* ends. Preparation for war may not serve merely the goals of national defenses, but, as has often occurred in the past, may produce attitudes and beliefs which cause war. Reliance on the threat of annihilation may create conditions which make annihilation necessary. Unconventional wisdom looks beyond the formal structure to examine the informal structure, for it believes, among other things, in the existence of self-fulfilling prophecies.

The way in which one frames a problem limits the possibilities of its solution. Saul Friedman in his study of RAND, a civilian research arm of the Air Force, found that the organization "has done little positive research toward ending nuclear confrontation because of the belief of RAND's leading thinkers that the theory of 'mutual invulnerability' is a positive way to peace." This is a conventional perception of the world, yet the danger of such narrow framing of problems is that research limited to this narrow perspective may influence political policy. The danger in this case was well founded, for in 1957 RAND predicted a Russian crash program in ICBM development, consistent with the military metaphysic of their client. The prediction was incorrect, but it encouraged the United States to embark on a crash program. By 1961, when it became evident to the

Russians that the United States had an overwhelming superiority, the Russians did increase their production of ICBMs. Friedman says: "The RAND prediction, as it turned out, precipitated another round of the arms race."[1]

The RAND incident is neither unique nor isolated. The particular incident is not of central importance. What is most important is its illustration of the process of the self-fulfilling prophecy. This process is not taken into account in the bulk of decision-making, even though it will largely determine the kind of world we will have or will not have tomorrow.

The self-fulfilling prophecy can be further illustrated. Young men are drafted into military service because of the "requirements" of national *defense*. When they get into the armed forces they are taught *war,* with its various arts, sciences, beliefs, and attitudes. It is thought that learning to wage war is an unfortunate necessity in keeping the peace. This way of framing the problem does not admit that military forces can be used for aggression or to pressure other nations into economic and political subservience. Even the label "Department of Defense" is a euphemism in support of the official function. (It was more accurately labeled the War Department a couple of decades ago.) So when our Marines land, as they did recently in the Dominican Republic, and as they have in many periods of American history, tortured rationalization is applied to call the act national defense.

Cloaking the armed forces in the role of national defense obscures much of what is taught by the military establishment. Ordinarily we think of "education" as formal schooling. Yet evidence strongly suggests that the pervasive qualities of an environment are more potent determiners of attitudes, values, beliefs, and behavior than formal classes labeled "education." When our government officials decide to draft young men into the armed forces they seldom treat it as compulsory education. National defense and manpower requirements are cited as the central issues. But the hard fact is that young men are sent into two or more years of compulsory war indoctrination.

Armed forces education seeks to build fighting morale by teaching a special military ideology which filters ideas and information.[2] Information is selected to fit the morale objectives. Descriptions of "enemy" powers are constructed to promote a fanatic fighting psychology. The metaphysical certainty of the military ideology provides a basis for unequivocal pronouncements, even in official materials, about the true meaning of human nature, freedom, the American way of life, and good and bad economic systems. The training goes well beyond teaching men how to fight. It tells them what to believe and why they should fight. The message is even reinforced by the Chaplain's Corps, which rationalizes the need to kill and provides divine sanction for each military adventure.

Such education assumes first that the indoctrination of beliefs and attitudes is necessary for national survival. But thought control is necessary only when the general reasons for fighting will not meet the test of open inquiry. Second, this education implies that the end justifies the means. This is true only within a system that has abandoned the democratic belief in the worth of the individual. When military training is seen as an educational system the anomaly becomes clear, for the American armed forces provide an education suitable more for a totalitarian society than for a democratic society.

Morris Janowitz points out that "military mission is the key to military organization.... The unique character of the military establishment derives from the requirement that its members are specialists in making use of violence and mass destruction."[3] The organization and management of violence excludes training in nonviolent conflict resolution and in determining the conditions under which violence might be defensible. Education in the military is education for learning to want to kill and how to kill. An education which emphasizes preparation for war as the only plausible alternative is likely to create its own world. Though the atomic age requires peace education, the lion's share of national wealth goes into a system which claims that thinking war is the only way to peace, and the message is even transmitted through a burgeoning international network of military radio stations.

Civilian War Education

War education, however, is not monopolized by the military. American television glorifies war for the young and the old, and American industry has shown the know-how to capitalize on the mass production of war toys and war games for American children. Divisive ethnocentrism and moralistic self-righteousness permeate television war stories and war games. It becomes normal and exciting to see the dehumanized enemy killed. Even in the Vietnam War the real thing became the game, and the mass media paraded statistics (often of dubious accuracy) on the daily kill. A high score of kills of the enemy produces delight; high scores against our side are lamented.

As American culture becomes more war-oriented, the value system of the armed forces often becomes a model for the American way of life. President Truman after World War II wanted universal military training "to develop citizenship responsibilities and to foster the moral and spiritual welfare of our young people."[4] And in 1964 Congress expanded the high school ROTC programs by nearly 500 percent, even though the Department of Defense said it was actually a hindrance to national defense. It was defended for its "educational" values, and there was scarcely any opposition, even from professional educators. Some educators even actively supported the program.

Our concern for appropriate educational experience has lagged far behind our national concern for military technology because the implications of the new technology are not adequately understood. The atomic and hydrogen bombs and their new delivery systems made most of the old weapons and old strategies obsolete. Everyone grants this, but what is typically not understood is that the old military *structures* are obsolete. Not only do they gobble up national resources and hinder economic improvement and social reform, but nation-states with massive atomic power have neither the capacity to produce successful aggression nor defense.

Smaller wars, such as those in Vietnam, no longer are worth the risk of escalation into thermonuclear disaster. A strong international police force under the United Nations is necessary to resolve violent conflicts, but national armed forces are obsolete. We now are developing a world comparable to a United States where the president has a small conventional military force and the governors of each state have nuclear power. To be sure, other nations would need to cooperate in disarming, but the failure to change cannot be blamed solely on other nations, for we do not lead disarmament policy.

The political implications of modern military technology are rarely comprehended by the professional militarists, so education within our national military establishment perpetuates the pre-atomic structure. It is an anachronistic education, therefore part of the problem rather than part of the solution. Those caught up in the burgeoning military establishment of World War II and the subsequent hot and cold wars have become the least likely to create a world without atomic holocaust. Yet those locked in the military value system constitute the core of the American establishment, whether they are nominally civilian or military. Life within a military establishment may be more charged with military values, but the expanding military-industrial-cultural complex has made the militaristic outlook a pervasive feature even of civilian culture. Nationalistic militarism, like all systems of belief, cannot be contained merely because a civilian president is commander-in-chief of the armed forces. Nations take on the characteristics of the enterprise they become involved in. We become what we do.

It is doubtful that the expanding militarization of American society can long continue without catastrophe, for a garrison state can hardly be expected to concentrate on the urgent goals of peace. C. Wright Mills has pointed out that the main cause of World War III will be preparation for war. We cannot blissfully continue to ignore the consequences of the attitudes and beliefs that war education produces.

Public School Peace Education

Public schools are among the institutions which usually reinforce conventional, pre-atomic "wisdom." To help prepare students for the atomic age, however, they could point out that the established outlook and the mass media which usually support such an outlook are representative of a traditional point of view. The school could help students examine unconventional alternatives and compare them with established orthodoxy. History could be studied culturally and the strains of violence and the war culture could be identified in the same way that a culture of poverty is now being identified. Education could focus on cross-cultural education and cross-cultural experience, especially with nations as important to the future as Russia and China. Issues of war and peace could take a more central role, while war indoctrination programs such as Junior ROTC would need to be discontinued. If military recruiters are permitted in the schools, the need for the students to know nonmilitary information should also be respected. Those who can explain the laws and procedures for conscientious objectors should be made equally available.

Pre-atomic thinking still permeates not only our schools and the armed forces but virtually all American institutions, yet our age urgently requires more planning based on reflective thought about where we have been, where we are going, and where we want to go. A few people are beginning to question whether our deterrence strategy really deters and whether our national defense defends. The unconventional wisdom emerging from such inquiry may offer solutions difficult to accept for those who are dependent on the beliefs of a pre-atomic world. Yet the option is not whether to reassess but when to reassess, and the kind of education Americans receive or fail to receive will affect their capacities to choose. Basic reassessment will come, but it would be more useful prior to World War III than afterwards.

Notes

[1] Saul Friedman, "The RAND Corporation and Our Policy Makers," *The Atlantic,* September, 1963, p. 68.

[2] See William Boyer, "The Armed Forces as Educator," *Proceedings of the Philosophy of Education Society,* 1963, pp. 85-92.

[3] Morris Janowitz, *Sociology and the Military Establishment.* New York: Russell Sage Foundation (for the American Sociology Society), 1959, p. 106.

[4] Harry S. Truman, *Memoirs.* New York: Doubleday, 1955, Vol. 1, p. 511.

Chapter Eighteen

Junior ROTC:
Militarism in the Schools

> *By confusing democratic education with military training,*
> *public schools often train people*
> *to be warriors rather than citizens.*

Obsessive anti-communism in the United States has helped confuse ideological issues by treating communism as the basic ideological opponent of American society. If American society affirms democratic values, totalitarianism is in basic ideological opposition, and the ideological opposition to communism should be based primarily on its totalitarian features.

Totalitarian values need not be restricted to government—they can include institutional structures and interpersonal relations throughout the society. Institutions can establish patterns which predispose interpersonal relations toward either democratic or totalitarian values. Complex institutions would be expected to reveal varying degrees of both democratic and totalitarian values, yet the relative emphasis becomes crucial, especially in schools responsible for preparation of youth for citizenship in that society.

Former President Dwight Eisenhower, in his well-known farewell address of January 17, 1961, [1] warned that "...we must guard against the acquisition of unwarranted influence, whether sought or unsought, by the military-industrial complex." He pointed out that "...the total influence—economic, political, even spiritual—is felt in every city, every statehouse, every office of the federal government."

The influence of the military in and on education is also part of the general military complex which is becoming normalized and therefore institutionalized. The purpose of this study is to identify some of the ways in which militarism is involved in the schools. Junior ROTC will be given central attention and ideological characteristics of military values will be analyzed.

Education's Response to an Expanding Military

Teachers old enough to remember life before World War II are often surprised to find that their students accept an expanded military and a compulsory military draft as a normal part of the American way of life. They sometimes fail to realize that today's student knows life only since World War II. The "warfare state" is his only frame of reference.[2] A citizen living during the 1930s would have been more likely to offer resistance and even to use the label "police state" if he had been asked to give up six to eight years to the military, part in active service and part in a reserve unit. Current "peacetime" military requirements call for more years of "service" than those of the period in which most World War II veterans served. In some areas, public high schools require two years of compulsory ROTC, with two years more required at the state university, and the student is still subject to the draft. Employers often treat job applicants who have not completed their military "obligations" as second-rate candidates, since they could be taken at any time by the military. This discrimination has provided a coercive economic inducement to complete military service.

Not only has American society become increasingly tolerant of militarism since World War II, the military has become increasingly idolized and sacrosanct. In a study of high school teachers conducted in the mid-1950s, the statement, "We need to build a stronger military force," was consistently selected among a large variety of potentially controversial statements as the statement which was least controversial. The majority of teachers thought they would risk their positions if they dared to advocate or even to discuss impartially in the classroom the question of "Elimination of the 'flag salute.'" However, virtually all teachers thought that they could either advocate or use for classroom study the assertion, "We need to build a stronger military force."[3]

Also, in a 1957 study of high school students in a metropolitan area, students were asked to offer criticisms of the world as they saw it. A wide variety of statements was offered, but none included objections to military conscription.[4]

It is a well-known sociological principle that *means* instituted on a temporary basis, such as an expanded post-war military, easily becomes institutionalized and treated as *ends*. The emergency measure becomes part of a way of life, fully adorned with myth and rationalization.

The Purpose of Militarism

The military is an instrument of violence controlled by the state. Though such an instrument may be needed under certain circumstances, it must be recognized that it is an instrument embracing what is essentially despicable. Violence might be defended as an unavoidable last resort in a defensive action against others who use violence, but this is not to condone violence. It is only to make use of it when no nonviolent alternative is available. When men defend violence itself, they have taken on the "morality" of the psychopath. Should such sanction become widespread, civilization will have sunk to its lowest depths. The Nazis revered militarism as a means and as an end. It was logical that they should, for their belief that right was based on might led to military idolization.

This does not mean that a democratic state in a non-internationally organized world should be without any armed forces, but it does mean that the armed forces must be recognized for what they are, and their central values must never become the central values of that democratic state. When the military becomes coupled to an educational institution, the essential military commitment is easily ignored. The real goals of institutions are determined by what the institutions do; therefore, ROTC in the high school raises serious questions about the purposes of the alleged "educational" institutions. When ROTC is compulsory, the institution indicates that it has not only accommodated ROTC but has even given priority to military values. To require a course is a way of indicating that it is so high on the hierarchy of values of that institution that it cannot be left to the elective choice of the student.

Junior ROTC

The relationship between religion and public education has long been a topic of dispute, whereas the relationship between militarism and public education, which probably raises more serious questions, has received virtually no public attention. In fact, many people are not even aware that there are military programs in public schools.

Junior ROTC programs are used in 242 public high schools and 10 private high schools. Programs are *compulsory* in 46 public high schools. The programs are nearly all in large city schools and they enroll approximately 60,000 students.

Number of Junior ROTC Programs in the United States

	Public High Schools	Private High Schools
Required	46	9
Elective	196	1
Total	242	10

Typically, words such as "discipline," "leadership," "patriotism," and "respect" are associated with ROTC programs to justify acceptance in the schools. Rarely is there any indication that such value-laden words can have a number of different meanings. However, there are at least two very different ways of evaluating the educational meaning of ROTC programs—one through a totalitarian frame of reference, the other through a democratic frame of reference. In the evaluation of these programs, "totalitarian" will be used to refer primarily to a process by which people are taught to define themselves by uncritically accepting an imposed pattern of behavior and belief. "Democratic" will refer primarily to a process by which people are taught to define themselves through critical social interaction and to participate in the formation of the rules they follow.

The following allegations are commonly advanced by supporters of Junior ROTC programs. For each of these a rebuttal is submitted.

1. *ROTC programs help discipline students, and young people in American society are in need of discipline.*

The aim "to instill discipline" is stated in the official Junior ROTC *Program of Instruction*.[5] The word *instill* should be noted. The emphasis on discipline as uncritical acceptance is further confirmed by the statement that teaching of discipline should include "Drill of foot troops including squad, platoon, and company drill. Wearing of the uniform. Duties of the individual soldier."[6]

Neither the above allegation nor the *Program of Instruction* distinguishes between two very different forms of discipline. One is self-discipline guided by intelligence; the other is uncritical acceptance of imposed demands. The first is "democratic" discipline; the second is "totalitarian." Military discipline stresses the latter type. What is condoned is *regimentation* of body and mind. The disciplined soldier obeys not unlike Pavlov's dog, and the modern army's still-coveted use of drill provides a useful procedure for producing this type of discipline. Orders are not meant to be food for thought but uncritically accepted directives for action.

Some teachers within the professional faculty of a public school may also equate discipline with regimentation, but such teachers are anomalies in a democratically oriented profession. The ROTC instructor, who is a member of the armed forces, is employed precisely *because* he will use regimentation to effect discipline. He is obligated to effect values which are essentially totalitarian, and so to the degree that schools are committed to the democratically oriented goals of intellectual self-discipline, ROTC is a subverting influence.

2. *High School ROTC produces urgently needed military leadership.*

Secretary of Defense McNamara testified before the Housed Armed Services Committee that "the program has failed to produce adequate numbers of officers," and that Junior ROTC cannot be justified on this basis.

Even if it were shown that Junior ROTC aided in producing military leadership, the argument for having Junior ROTC would not be sufficient. American public schools should be centrally committed to the democratic values of the larger society, a task which is sufficiently difficult even when schools are not sidetracked with ancillary functions. Schools cannot justify the inclusion of programs which seriously conflict with their avowed central aims.

3. *Officer training in ROTC develops the general qualities of leadership. ROTC is the training ground for tomorrow's leaders, not only in the armed forces but also in private enterprise and government.*

The Junior ROTC *Program of Instruction* does specify that "training in leadership...will be progressive throughout the three-year program." The following example is offered: "Develop leadership qualities through individual exercise of command and conduct of drill. Students will conduct drill and perform in command positions. To obtain desired results, precision and accuracy of every movement in each exercise will be stressed."[7]

What conception of leadership is implicit in this military model?[8] *Command* and *drill* are terms offered to characterize the view. A command in a drill situation is an absolute order moving from the commander to the performer. The command is to be performed with maximum "precision and accuracy." The performer is to do what he is told without questioning whether the order is justified. The implied product of such leadership is the automaton.

This leadership is the leadership of the puppetmaster, who leads by pulling and pushing the verbal conditioned response strings he has tied to the followers. His leadership is assigned, and he is called on to divest himself of as much of his individuality as are the followers. He too must take a follower's role at times, for the military view is "to give orders, you first must know how to take them."[9]

Once again there is the totalitarian view, in this case underlying the military conception of leadership. A democratic frame of reference produces an antithetical conception of leadership. The purpose of democratic leadership is not to eliminate individuality but to increase it—not to build uncritical conditioned responses but to develop critical interaction. Democratic leadership is functional and changing, not designated and rigid, and it is characterized by its ability to help people develop shared interests and examine group goals.

The simple, mechanistic, totalitarian model of leadership specified by the Junior ROTC Program conflicts with the more complicated, humanistic, democratic model of leadership. No school can make sense of an equal commitment to both conceptions of leadership.

4. *Schools fail to develop patriotism and ROTC helps to fill this need.*
The Junior ROTC *Program of Instruction* explicitly states that one objective is "to develop patriotism."[10] Military organizations com-

monly emphasize patriotic allegiance, since they serve the role of protector of the state. But once again it is necessary to avoid a singular meaning. As with the concepts of *discipline* and *leadership,* it is necessary to distinguish between two very different means of patriotism.

Nationalism, in varying degrees of intensity, represents one kind of patriotism. It is developed by stressing some form of indiscriminate worship of the state, ranging from uncritical acceptance to jingoistic chauvinism. The teacher of nationalism should propagandize so that an uncritical emotional attachment to the state is developed which encourages the individual to define himself by his nationalistic identification (e.g., I *am* an American, or a German, or a Japanese," etc.). This is the conception of patriotism stressed by the military,[11] one which is essentially totalitarian.

The democratic conception of patriotism treats the state as the product of the critical political participation of the members of the society. Loyalty is primarily to the human race and the democratic process, and so loyalty to a particular state is not blind loyalty to any myth of the state. No attempt is made to worship "my country, right or wrong," though appreciation and depreciation are inevitably the outcome of a study of the country in which one lives. The democratic method involves *study* rather than indoctrination, for *understanding* is considered to be more important than nationalistic piety. Democratic patriotism does not encourage ethnocentrism nor a divisive belief in the superiority of one's own nation over another. The democratic method, its commitment to the method of intelligence, and a critical appreciation of one's country based on honest study are the elements of democratic patriotism. For a school to teach the military form of patriotism is to commit the school to values underlying a totalitarian ideology and to use the schools to help defeat the kind of patriotism which is the foundation of a democratic society.

5. American citizens often do not show sufficient respect for authority; therefore, ROTC programs help develop better citizens by teaching respect for authority.

A stated objective of the Junior ROTC *Program of Instruction* is to teach "respect for constituted authority."[12] There is no indication that the kind of authority one should respect should be democratically constituted authority.

The American trials of German prisoners after World War II were premised on the assumption that one should *not* respect non-demo-cratically constituted authority. The willingness of Germans to obey imposed authority is considered a cause of World War II; therefore, the American military teaches a totalitarian concept of authority that has been rejected by the American judicial system and is considered to be a cause of the most disastrous war in the history of man.

6. *Armed forces training is basically a process of teaching; therefore, ROTC instructors, who have undergone armed forces training, are adequately prepared to teach in a public school.*

The term *professional* used in the phrase *professional soldier* does not have the same meaning as *professional* when it is describing a *professional educator.* A professional educator has a specialization and the Junior ROTC instructor also possesses this qualification. But the professional educator is probably different in every other way. He has a broad academic background, knowledge of educational psychology, and usually some understanding of the social and philosophical foundations of education. These areas of preparation are intellectual prerequisites of an educator as distinguished from a trainer. The preparation of the professional educator is designed to help him to free the student intellectually and to help humanize the student through a broad understanding of human experience. An educator can take account of many frames of reference to aid a student in approaching problems in different ways. The professional educator has been prepared to help students be inquiring and participating members in the intelligent improvement of the society.

The Junior ROTC instructor does not serve primarily the role of an educator who emphasizes understanding but more the role of a trainer, a salesman, and a propagandist. He is told to "inspire, motivate, and interest the student in ROTC and the Army, and to establish a lasting sense of the Army's contribution to the nation."[13] Junior ROTC instructors are in an extra-professional role which exempts them from normal controls through certification and also from the standards of ethics and academic freedom central to the profession.

Therefore, Junior ROTC instructors do not meet the standards of preparation normally expected of public school teachers. If the professional standards of the teacher are necessary to qualify the teacher for his role, the armed forces instructor is not qualified to teach in a public school. The preparation of the armed forces instructor may be appropriate to instruction in a military institution. To include the armed forces instructor in a system of professional public education is to forfeit those protections for students which have been built into the certification requirements for teachers. For the public schools to treat the armed forces instructor as qualified to teach is to imply that the academic and intellectual prerequisites for the certification of the qualified teacher are superfluous.

7. *The instructional budget is supplemented through use of armed forces instructors; therefore, a Junior ROTC program eases the cost of instruction to the taxpayer.*

An argument for Junior ROTC based primarily on economy would equally justify Communists or Fascists on the teaching staff under the pay of a foreign government, hardly a compelling logical extension of the argument if one asks for economy at any price. An economy proposal which ignores educational values defeats the basis for a school system.

Even if one should disregard educational values, the argument that the taxpayer is relieved is still specious. The funds are simply channeled through federal instead of local taxes. This argument is illusory and represents a provincial view of fiscal responsibility.

Armed Forces Guidance in the Schools

The armed forces seem to be willing to influence any aspect of the public schools. In 1960 the Air Force pamphlet titled *The Struggle for Men's Minds* was sent to public school counselors for the stated purpose of getting counselors to "help students maintain ability and will to fight."[14] The pamphlet is prefaced by a quotation which includes the statement, "Every society has a right to...prohibit the propagation of opinions which have a dangerous tendency.... No member of society has a right to teach any doctrine contrary to what the society holds to be true."[15] This statement denies the concept of academic freedom, which is based on the democratic concept of free speech translated into teaching as freedom of inquiry and, therefore, freedom to learn.

There is not only the problem of the totalitarian implications of the armed forces' publications but also the problem of inaccuracy which is likely to result when materials are developed by those who may not be academically qualified in the area in which they write. The above pamphlet includes a letter addressed "to the School Counselor" from an Air Force lieutenant colonel. Written three years after the Russian Communists affirmed a policy of co-existence with the West, it states: "...there cannot be co-existence of democracy and communism and the struggle is inevitably a mortal one."[16]

The Confusion of Aims

Teachers can obtain exemption from the draft, a special privilege which may help make them feel obligated and less free to make critical evaluations of the military. Teachers are also often members of military reserves, using the reduced prices of clubs and PXs, free air travel, and other privileged subsidies. They therefore develop a dependence, with attendant obligations, on an institution largely characterized by values antithetical to those democratic values to which they are ostensibly committed.

Military influence in the schools should not be attributed solely to armed forces policy. In many schools this influence has been accepted, even welcomed, with little or no recognition of the conflict between military values and the values one would expect to characterize public schools in a democracy. This acceptance raises such questions as: Are democratic values and military values really in opposition? If so, are there any central aims in these high schools with ROTC programs? If there are central aims, are they so similar to military aims that conflict is avoided?

Other Considerations

In this brief study many considerations must be omitted. Nothing has been said, for example, of high school-sponsored military recruiting programs or the distribution of military propaganda through the schools. More needs to be said about the military use of uniforms, serial numbers, ranks, haircut uniformity, and the planned dehumanization and destruction of individuality built into these procedures. The feudal remnants of a two-class social system, which is still used by the military, deserves consideration.

The armed forces may know what is necessary to carry on warfare, but they uphold a system of beliefs (possibly necessary for warfare) which is alien to the democratic values of the larger society. When militarism ceases to be tightly contained as a system serving democratic values, it becomes a threat to the values—and possibly even to the existence—of the society that supports it.

In a time when more highly qualified teachers are required, when federal aid for normal education is desperately needed, the federal government supplies the schools with soldier-teachers. It is widely acknowledged that students need increasingly competent teachers to help them understand the crucial issues of our ever more complicated and dangerous world. Proposals are even being made to lengthen the school day or add to the school year, since the normal school program is assumed to be too short. Yet 60,000 students spend part of their current high school program in the most anti-intellectual form of activity—marching and learning to accept regimentation.

Such common acceptance of military influences, particularly incorporation of Junior ROTC into the high school curriculum, illuminates the philosophical confusion of much current education. With latent and overt violence already a threatening feature of American life, it is paradoxical, to say the least, that so many American public schools should embrace military values.

If the defense department really wishes to economize; if the U.S. Office of Education really wishes to avoid federal control of the public school curriculum; and if public high schools really accept intellect-centered, democratic aims (instead of anti-intellectual-indoctrinational-totalitarian aims)—then all Junior ROTC programs should be terminated as soon as possible.

Notes

This article alerted the education community in the 1960s. By the 1990s such programs had *expanded* to 2,900 high schools and 290,000 students, paid through the "peace dividend."

[1] Dwight D. Eisenhower, "Liberty Is at Stake," *Vital Speeches,* February 1, 1961, p. 229.

[2] Fred Cook, *The Warfare State.* New York: The Macmillan Company, 1962.

[3] William H. Boyer, "Conformity Implications of Certain Current Secondary Educational Theories." Unpublished dissertation, Arizona State University, 1956, pp. 194-204.

4 William H. Boyer, "Attitudes, Opinions, and Objectives of High School Students in the Milwaukee Area," *Journal of Educational Sociology,* March, 1959, p. 347.

5 Program of Instruction for Junior Division Reserve Officers Training Corps, ATP 145-4, p. 1.

6 *Ibid.,* p. 5.

7 *Ibid.,* pp. 5-6.

8 See also *Military Leadership,* Department of the Army, FM 22-100, June, 1961.

9 *The Soldier's Guide.* Washington: Department of the Army, FM 21-12, August, 1961, p. 138.

10 "Program," *op. cit.,* p. 1.

11 Cf. *The U.S. Fighting Man's Code.* Washington: DOD PAM 1-16, 1959, pp. 87-88, 100-104.

12 "Program," *op. cit.,* p. 1.

13 *Ibid.*

14 Paul E. Torrance, *The Struggle for Men's Minds.* Washington: USAF, 1960, p. 98.

15 *Ibid.,* "Introduction," listed as a quote from "_____ Johnson."

16 *Ibid.,* p. 105.

Chapter Nineteen

Misunderstanding Defense

*Television programs often convey
the pre-atomic model of national defense,
which hinders the public from considering
effective forms of national security in the nuclear age.*

The five-hour CBS TV series in the mid-1980s on American national defense was an educational disaster. The programs focused on what we still call "defense" and on better understanding of the Soviet perspective, but they neither recognized war as a political system nor suggested the obsolescence of military-based defense in the atomic age.

National security is possible in the atomic age through an international or supra-national system but not by merely adding money, technology, or people to the old national system. Expanding the military is the formula for increasing the arms race, escalating overkill, and reducing countries such as the United States to radioactive rubble.

The first error is to assume that the central problem is Russia or communism. The Vietnam War had nothing to do with Russia. The wars between Israel and Arab countries probably would have occurred if Russia and communism did not exist.

The second error is the failure to understand that specific wars are incidents of a particular institution—the war system. War is the result of legitimizing national sovereignty and military power as the ultimate authority in international relations. If there is no formal judicial system of world law and no supporting police force, the *absence* of a system of law and order perpetuates the old war system, based on global anarchy.

Violence can be managed and reduced by creating the same set of international institutions normally used within a nation: mediation, public communication, adjudication, police action, and responsive legislation which addresses economic injustices.

The human race has survived precariously under the old war system as the technology of military violence has increased exponentially, but now with atomic weapons the price is not only too high but the system has collapsed. The United States and Russia have a "defense" system in name only. It cannot defend. It can only produce aggression and mutual annihilation when war occurs with a nuclear power.

Word magic does not help, whether in changing the name of the War Department to the Defense Department after World War II, or in labeling a missile an "anti-missile missile," or in having a "civil defense" program.

Our "deterrence" system works, as President John Kennedy pointed out with irony, except when there is "accident, miscalculation, or madness," all normal features of the international system. One might add that third-party nuclear intervention can also be used surreptitiously to get two nuclear nations to destroy themselves. And the more nuclear powers, the greater the instability.

Changes in the international system can best be initiated by major nations such as the United States, but the United States has no policy to help transform the war system. After World War II when the World Court was about to develop, the United States crippled it through the Connally amendment which excluded "court jurisdiction over matters within the domestic jurisdiction of the United States as determined by the United States."

This self-judging clause was then used by other nations and assured the impotence of the court. If the United States had been brought to the World Court for intervention in Vietnam, it could nullify the action by claiming the conflict was a domestic issue.

Too few Americans, including apparently Dan Rather and Walter Cronkite of CBS, understand the way the rules of the international game have created the war system nor what the alternatives are for having national security in the atomic age. This conceptual tunnel helps reinforce the military-industrial complex and helps make World War III a self-fulfilling prophecy, accelerated under the Reagan administration.

We do not have to behave like lemmings, but, since we are not genetically programmed for disaster, we need to use intelligence for institutional change rather than merely strengthening obsolete institutions by adding more technology and people.

George Kennan proposes a 50 percent reduction in strategic arms as a first step in reducing overkill. A larger set of such unilateral and multilateral possibilities is also available. A recent Gallup Poll indicates that Americans would support nuclear disarmament by a 2 to 1 margin.

The task is now to design an international peace-keeping system which would be phased in simultaneous to phasing down the national military system and to provide international leadership toward the cooperation of nations.

The odds for catastrophic war would be greatly reduced and the benefits in employment, inflation reduction, and reduced taxes could be significant.

Chapter Twenty

World Order Education:
What Is It?

> *World order education should be*
> *a standard part of the social studies curriculum*
> *to help people design necessary 21st Century institutions.*

Only a few decades ago world order education was virtually unheard of. But the 1960s saw rapid worldwide development of peace research and theories of war prevention. Courses in peace studies began in a number of institutions throughout the world, especially in Europe and North America. By 1974, 29 undergraduate institutions of higher education in the United States offered an academic major or a certificate in peace studies.

World order studies are a special variety of peace studies. Particularly because of the efforts of the Institute for World Order, an academic field of world order education has developed which is rapidly incorporating a substantial body of literature and research, including courses in teacher education and other disciplines. World order workshops are increasingly commonplace at curriculum conferences and social studies meetings, and the National Council for the Social Studies has recognized peace education and world order education as a legitimate part of the social studies program. Yet few educators and fewer of the general public know what "world order education" means.

World order education is an upgraded form of political education. It is citizenship education which transcends the nationalistic and pre-ecological values of the old citizenship education. It is global in outlook, human-value-centered, problem solving, and futurist. Its closest kin, international education, has been primarily descriptive, using conventional academic methodology to describe and explain the present world. As a result, it has been nation-state-centered, value neutral, and concerned centrally with understanding the present rather than creating a better future. World order education, by contrast, is solution-centered. Therefore, it is an instrument of social-cultural change.

Its first and continuing commitment is to aid in eliminating the institution of war. But there is a broader commitment toward world planning and the creation of global institutions better able to serve human needs in this precarious and yet potentially promising period of human history. In the development of such change, the nation-state is identified as only one possible "actor," and central consideration is given to the importance of other transnational and supranational alternatives.

Transnational behavior consists of rapidly developing links among people throughout the world. Professional and scholarly organizations are increasingly transnational. As communication increases, common cross-national interests can be identified and a new network of human organizations can be developed. Such transnational groups exert a new dimension of *political* influence.

Supranational authority can be created to control nations in the same way that federal law limits state law. A world political/legal system can have authority which supersedes the nation-state in specific areas, limiting national sovereignty and widening the implementation of the institution of law.

Overcoming the Value Dilemma

Western scholarship is grounded in tradition stemming from the Greeks, who considered knowledge to be an end in itself. This frame of reference led scholars to detach themselves from the application of knowledge and to be concerned only with "truth" and logic. As a consequence, scholarship and research became detached from the affairs of life, and political eunuchism became the price of scholarship in the same way that celibacy became the price of entering the priesthood. To fill the need created by modern industrial society, the world soon had two kinds of thinkers: those who pursued abstract knowledge unrelated to life and those who pursued short-range, practical applications of technical knowledge. This dichotomy left a vacuum at the most critical point, where knowledge was applied to the common problems of people—the problems of war, poverty, economic instability, political justice, and more recently threats to the ecological life-support system.

Many leaders have addressed themselves to the need to make this transition. Social philosophers ranging from Marx to Dewey have tried during this last century to tie knowledge and value into a public philosophy.

Saul Mendlovitz, a lawyer and sociologist at Rutgers University, addressed himself to this same problem during the early 1960s in connection with the development of a more effective theory of war prevention. He sought to find a defensible way in which research and education could contribute to the solution of a problem that had, in the atomic age, become a threat to the continuation of human life. He understood the absurdity of pursuing knowledge, yet ignoring the existence of problems that could liquidate humanity.

Grenville Clark and Louis B. Sohn's monumental *World Peace through World Law* suggested a research and teaching model that could contribute to the needed transformation. They had developed a plan for the transformation of the United Nations that took account of the need for disarmament, peace keeping, economic development, and the redistribution of political power. It provided a 10-year incremental transition period and included ingenious ways to substitute one security system for another without creating unacceptable insecurity for nations at any point during the transition.

Mendlovitz not only understood that the Clark-Sohn proposal was an excellent contribution to the design of institutional transformation, but that the design process it incorporated was a key to a different form of scholarship. Why not retain some elements of the utopian tradition and turn them into practical planning instruments for guiding social change? Even though most utopian planning has been elitist and impractical, why not create an approach to education and research that made broad social designs into directional tools for social change? After all, if we do not decide where we want to go, how are we to get there?

The forecasting techniques of the 1950s and 1960s were providing information that made it clear that the drift of trends was suicidal. The atomic war system would lead to atomic war, the economic maldistribution system would lead to even greater poverty, and the most recent ecological projections showed that our use and abuse of the environment was equally catastrophic.

So if the present system is impractical and even suicidal and immoral, wouldn't integrated, democratized global planning be the sane and responsible alternative? And if our traditional neutralist approach to research and education keeps the old order intact, isn't a new approach to research and education required to build a new world order?

Mendlovitz understood that the continued survival of the human species on this planet could only occur because the anarchy of nation-state sovereignty in the present world system had come under a more rational form of management. But that form of management could be either totalitarian and oppressive or democratic and representative. He recognized that we can have both survival and justice only if we get to work as scientists, scholars, citizens, and educators and transform key institutions by planning the direction of global social change.

His own initiatives began with a joint project with Richard Falk which resulted in a five-volume *Strategy for World Order* series that collated pertinent world order materials and showed the difficulty of creating a new world order. It was sponsored by the Institute for World Order, then called the World Law Fund, an organization resulting from Mendlovitz's meeting with a kindred spirit from the business world, Harry Hollins, who helped bring the organization into being. Since then the Institute for World Order and its expanding team of directors and consultants has constituted one of the most important instruments for giving stimulus and focus to the development of world order studies.

The Institute for World Order then sponsored Mendlovitz's second ambitious project: organizing project directors throughout the world to design models of a preferred world for the 1990s. This project, which provided fresh points of view from regional teams of scholars throughout the world, has now been completed. It constitutes a major contribution to global planning, and it contributes to *world interest* goals which make world order studies the kind of political-moral-educational activity that has helped solve the old indoctrination dilemma of value-centered education. By focusing on world interest goals instead of national goals or other special interest group goals, political education is raised to a world humanist level. These transnational human-centered goals exemplify the social application of the universal principle of the worth and dignity of the human person. By designing institutions that serve this core value, knowledge is used to help solve common problems that threaten human life and to contribute to cultural transformation which elevates the quality of human experience.

American schools have accepted the legitimacy of "affirmative action" with respect to race and sexual discrimination, despite some political infighting to the contrary. World order education has advanced the concept of affirmative action into other areas of educational inquiry, for it channels human intelligence into a search for solutions to unresolved public problems, solutions which are needed to affirm the principle of the worth and dignity of the individual. The institutional and social application of this principle results in the affirmation of such values as "peace, economic welfare, social justice, political participation, and ecological balance." World order studies focus on the development of research and education which help people find ways to analyze, clarify, and realize these values. In a world that generally does not serve such values, the neutral posture of conventional education often constitutes indirect political support of dangerous and dehumanizing institutions that are as inappropriate to the atomic and ecological age in which we live as chattel slavery was to America in the mid-Nineteenth Century.

Transition, Planning, Substitution

With the help of the Institute for World Order, its university-based centers, field consultants, and transnational programs, world order studies are being translated into curriculum materials and planning tools which are helping to involve students and the general public in the design and control of social change. The central goals are to raise the odds for collective human survival and social justice. Attention is given not only to planning goals but also to transition steps, and people throughout the world are increasingly participating in the design process. Simulation models and systems analysis are used as research and teaching vehicles with particular focus on world social, economic, political, and legal systems.

A system found to be sufficiently obsolete and pathological requires fundamental redesign rather than face-lifting; that system must be either eliminated or fundamentally transformed through substitution of a qualitatively different institution which does a better job of serving human needs. This involves designing a peace-keeping system in lieu of our present war system, an economic distribution system in lieu of our present maldistribution/poverty system, and an ecologically managed economy in lieu of the current pre-ecological exploitation/waste system.

Transferred into curriculum practice, this means examining alternative models of survival and social justice in relation to short, medium, and long-range planning. It means tying in local, national, regional, and global planning. It means helping people learn to control and transform their institutions instead of being controlled by them. It means re-examining institutional values and procedures that have been accepted without question.

We are beginning to understand how it is often easier to solve a number of social and ecological problems simultaneously rather than one at a time. We are also discovering that sensible short-range planning disconnected from long-range planning can often assure that the wrong thing will be done in the long run. Also, rational plans to serve a local community, developed in isolation from the larger society, often assure results contradictory to the larger public interest.

Systems analysis requires that we distinguish between natural systems and invented systems. Invented systems include social systems and technological systems. We have learned to be creative about the development of techno-systems while remaining largely closed to the transformation of social structures, e.g., political-economic systems. The effect has been progressively to use technology to exploit natural systems in order to serve traditional political-economic values. Such a society teaches people to serve institutions instead of teaching them to get their institutions to serve people.

Choice is the basic principle of human freedom, but in practice it usually means choice *within* existing social-political-economic systems. This works adequately when institutions are highly appropriate to the needs of an age. If they are not appropriate, "freedom" should become freedom to choose *between* institutional alternatives, which requires examination, exploration, and invention of alternative institutional systems. Though it is becoming increasingly popular to hear that the ecological crisis has made freedom obsolete, world order theorists such as those connected with the Institute for World Order take the opposite position and stress the need for public involvement in planning. They support the use of education to help people move for the first time in history toward control of their common destiny.

This new freedom precludes unilateral "freedom" to destroy the common life-support system and excludes freedom to develop structures that permit one group to exploit another. But in the trade-off, it opens up freedom to have a society choosing its destiny, based on interdependent cooperation and community. When choice over common policy is an orderly social-political enterprise, law, justice, and democracy have been institutionalized. The process can occur at local, national, and even global levels.

Participatory systemic planning is a basic tool to overcome our adherence to current systems. The military-industrial complex cannot be dismantled until there are guaranteed jobs in peace-oriented work. Management and labor will support the present system until there is a viable, rewarding, guaranteed alternative, and there can be no guaranteed alternative unless political power is used to implement a phased transition into a peace economy. Yet there is not likely to be such a plan without an international change in which the unavoidable anarchy of the nation-state is transformed into a world law system or a multilateral peace-keeping system providing real collective security. So a transition plan must be a long-range, phased, integrated plan which is supported by a politicized and planning-oriented citizenry. The United States has no such transition plan nor is there any indication that recent or current presidents, the secretaries of state, or the secretaries of defense have had any such plan in mind.

Our society seems to have two alternatives: either a continuation of the present cataclysmic war system until it self-destructs or the creation of a peace economy. Society can plan the transition or it can hope that an accident such as a small war will provide the necessary nudge. If the Vietnam War were considered a test case, the nudge hypothesis would fail, for the old arms race continues.

Waiting for the optimum accident is highly precarious, for it is likely to produce *both* massive destruction *and the reinstatement* of the war system, as the human remnants of a global war regress to primitive forms of group survival. The destruction of institutions without articulated plans for their replacement is a misplaced vision stemming from our failure to have learned planning appropriate to this new era. It explains many of the protest failures of the 1960s. So an essential form of knowledge for survival is systems change and transition planning, and this requires new public education.

But How Long Have We?

Back in 1969 when U Thant was asked this question, he gave the following reply:

> I do not wish to seem overdramatic, but I can only conclude from the information that is available to me as secretary-general that the members of the United Nations have perhaps 10 years left in which to subordinate their ancient quarrels and launch a global partnership to curb the arms race, to improve the human environment, to defuse the population explosion, and to supply the requisite momentum to development efforts.
>
> If such a global partnership is not forged within the next decade, then I very much fear that the problems I have mentioned will have reached such staggering proportions that they will be beyond our capacity to control.

Richard Falk held a slightly modified position during his recent work as director of the North American World Order Models Project for the Institute for World Order. He decided that unless we accomplish a basic systems change during this century we will probably have gone past the point of ecological no return, where overshoot will take an astronomical toll. Widespread atomic war can occur as long as the war system is intact, so the sooner there is global structural change the better.

However, such changes cannot occur overnight, and Falk proposed the following timetable: The 1970s need to be the decade of education, focusing on raising public consciousness. The 1980s should center on basic global planning to achieve agreement on objectives and a time schedule. The 1990s should realize basic minimal changes such as disarmament, development of an international peace-keeping system, and the creation of sufficient world law and government to provide some redress of the gap between the rich and the poor. A world ecological management system is equally necessary.

The lag is illuminated by recognition of the wide public support accorded Henry Kissinger, even though his approach is a short-range, ad hoc, bilateral, nineteenth-century balance-of-power kind of diplomacy. Meanwhile, the nuclear club expands, the arms race continues, and the world spends over 250 billion dollars a year to keep the system intact while human and environmental needs are neglected.

If Not World Order Education, What?

The theories of world order education now in use by the Institute for World Order and its cooperative educators, researchers, and consultants are not intended to close the doors to other theoretical approaches. Other plausible approaches to survival and social justice are welcome, and the models that have been developed are open and continually subjected to criticism and improvement. But they have been substantially tested through years of rigorous analysis and dialogue in the academic community, and those who object on substantive grounds ought to propose a better alternative. The possibilities for developing effective instructional vehicles have, however, barely been tapped.

The current need is therefore not primarily in the refinement of existing world order theory, though there is such a need, but in the typical curriculum which fails to include world order studies. Most teachers and most students have never confronted the urgency of our global problems, and even fewer have carefully explored and participated in the design of solutions.

The American student is pathetically uneducated for his role as a citizen of the world. It is unlikely that a person can be prepared to participate in solving global problems without first becoming involved in local planning. Most schools continue to assure the political illiteracy of their students even for local problems, and though young people can now vote at age 18 they are such foreigners to politics that they abdicate and continue to defer to the Establishment. Inadvertently, most schools help assure that the forecasts of the prophets of doom will become self-fulfilling prophecies.

Specifically, What Can We Do?

1. At the earliest age, help children develop:

a. *a social sense,* by cooperative play and association with mixed races, cultures, and economic levels;

b. *a political sense,* through participation in guiding some form of change in home, school, church, and other organizations; and

c. *an ecological sense,* by seeing the interdependence of plants and animals, by working with nature in a non-exploitative way, and by encouraging empathy and identification with all forms of life.

2. *Widen perspective toward a world view* geographically, ecologically, and culturally. Emphasize the use of globes rather than flags. Prepare the sequence of development so that a high school student will be able to design a United Nations II.

3. *Help students understand the direction of trends,* which includes the exponential consumption of nonrenewable resources, expansion of the nuclear arms race, population increases, and the widening gulf between underdeveloped and overdeveloped nations.

4. *Examine alternative futures,* comparative cultures, lifestyles, ideologies, economic systems, and world order models.

5. *Design preferred futures* by focusing on the question: What kind of society do you really want? Maximize the values of survival, social justice, and environmental quality with concrete illustration of what these values can mean.

6. *Test the feasibility of preferred models.* Identify trade-offs and transition steps. Identify ecological limits and the need for economic security.

7. *Treat a just society as a realistic society.* Put the burden of proof on those who want to justify the status quo. Transform the meaning of "realistic" so that it is equated with what ought to be done and can be done rather than with what is.

8. *Identify common problems and use the word "we" to refer to the human race.* Identify human needs and consensual goals. Focus on the solution to common world problems, and construct colleges and a world university based on such a curriculum. Align the schools with public interest and world interest and show how the two are becoming synonymous.

9. *Learn how to be politically effective.* Increase personal confidence through group social action. Begin with modest local goals, usually related to environment. Become involved in politics and community organization, and work with people engaged in planning and developing new legislation.

10. *Develop a futurist conception of identity.* Instead of the question "Who am I?" encourage "What do I want to become?" and "What kind of world do I want to live in and help create?" Use democratic group action as a basis for helping create identity.

11. *Contact the Institute for World Order* (formerly the World Law Fund) at 475 Riverside Drive, Room 246, New York, NY 10115, for direct assistance with program development, workshops, curriculum material, and as a clearinghouse for contact with people and organizations connected with world order education. Betty Reardon is director of peace education at Teachers College, Columbia University, New York, NY 10027.

Chapter Twenty-One

The De-Institutionalization of War

> *The war system was invented.*
> *It can be changed to a peace-keeping system.*
> *This requires intentional conversion of the war system*
> *and global institutions to enfore the rule of law.*

The Conventional Wisdom

Conventional wisdom treats the cause of war as either an event prior to the outbreak of war or a set of conditions that was antecedent to a war, which "caused" it.

Diplomacy is therefore to be used to prevent war when the set of conditions is expected to lead to war. (Unless the war is desired, then diplomacy can be a precipitator.)

Notice that this view presumes that what exists or has existed in the international system is the cause. We can call this "positive" causality, for an identifiable event or condition which is antecedent to the use of military violence is considered the "cause."

Can War Be Prevented?

If war is a random event, there is no way of predicting and stopping any particular war, therefore no way of preventing war from occurring. Most research on war has presumed that at least some predictability indicators are possible so that intervention might be used to prevent some wars. But the antecedent conditions that have occurred prior to wars and that may occur in the future to precipitate a war are exceedingly numerous. We move in the direction of identifying an infinite number of possible precipitating causes. One could even have a Freudian conception of the cause of why a head of state initiated war. And many possibilities exist if computers malfunction. The assumption that both prediction and successful war prevention intervention can reliably occur becomes a challenge to the human imagination. The need for achieving war prevention in the age of nuclear war requires a far more reliable way to prevent war, if such a way is available.

Is Peace Institutionalized?

Conventional wisdom presumes that peace is normal and that war is an aberration, a disturbance of the peace. But if war is normal and peace is an aberration, we can assume that war is either caused by human nature or by an international system which institutionalizes war.

If war were part of human nature, Colorado and Nebraska could be expected to go to war, unless their members were not human. But they are human and yet there is little chance of their going to war, so war in the international system must have a cause that does not exist between Colorado and Nebraska. The common language and even the economic interdependence between these states are not the distinguishing elements in their lack of war, for many countries with common languages and economic interdependence have gone to war. What is apparent is that any conflict serious enough to lead to violence between Colorado and Nebraska will be adjudicated in the institutionalized system of enforceable federal law, and the two states know that they do not need military forces for that very reason.

The illustration is typical of dispute settlement within civilized countries. Law is substituted for military power, and becomes ultimate authority. Yet, to date, in the international system the ultimate authority is military power. This is a de facto "war system." War is institutionalized, rather than peacekeeping, because peacekeeping has no formal authority. If Colorado and Nebraska had no federal dispute settlement system they might bring in a third party to engage in compulsory mediation. Use of their state militias would be another option. The relative size of the state militias might very well determine that decision, for those with more might are likely to opt for it being "right."

Positive and Negative Causality

Once we pose the question of the cause of war in general and we have difficulty finding a useful set of antecedent and precipitating causes which are positive events in the international system, we should ask whether the main cause of war is what is *lacking* in the international system. If we compare the international system with the *intra*national political units (Colorado and Nebraska) within a nation, it becomes clear that nations use law and the international system uses military violence. If what we have learned within nations is applied between nations, we can see that the main cause of war in general is *lack of any system of enforceable law in the international system.* So what is *not* there is the main determiner of the outcomes of international conflict. This is "negative causality."

Background of the War System

Humans invent their social systems, yet there was no time in history when the war system was intentionally created. Rather, there was no time in history when any political units were larger than a portion of the world. The international system consisted of anarchy by default.

By the 17th Century, the world had a number of nations, and because of lack of any *supra*national authority they settled their disputes through war when diplomacy failed, as it often did. When the long agonizing "Thirty Years' War" was settled in 1648 in Westphalia, there was growing interest in upgrading the international system, and the Peace of Westphalia produced a codification of new rules that were widely enough accepted to provide the basis for a code of "national sovereignty," diplomatic exchange, diplomatic privilege, retention of military power within nations for defense only, and cumulative international law.

The modern nation-state system was institutionalized, but the war system continued because there was no authority other than military-national violence, which continued to be ultimate authority. So the war system continued, producing exponentially increasing casualties in each war as military technology became more powerful. Now with nuclear power and at least 40 times the destructive power needed to produce nuclear winter, we have each nation-state reduced to impotence to prevent nuclear war. Global genocide is assured under the war system, and the only way to prevent it is to substitute supranational authority which can enforce settlements of conflict between nations without the use of war.

Supranational Authority

Supranational authority is rejected by many because the only image it conjures is monolithic repression—the police state writ large. Yet the authority that prevents Colorado and Nebraska from going to war is not based on monolithic repression. Representative law and justice is well understood within nations, and is the only acceptable alternative to the war system. The experience people have in controlling police power, providing divisions of power between executive and legislative branches, and in keeping decision-making sufficiently public to prevent dictatorial takeover can be applied to the international system. Even so, there are some risks of national military power, even with limited world law in place, for such law will require some form of armed police force. Yet the risk of *not* having law, in an age when the retention of national military power means the nuclearization of war, may be the *largest risk* the human race can take. Are we not now at the point where we must choose between global holocaust and the reduction of national sovereignty (though not its elimination)? Or will the "deterrence" theory prove sufficiently reliable so that we can actually rely on their being a future?

Nuclear Roulette

There is limited power to word magic, so to call a system a "deterrence system" does not make it so. The threat of nuclear retaliation sometimes deters, sometimes encourages a first strike, because a deterrence system looks different from the other side. It can be credited with deterring even though the other side had no need to be deterred. It is often claimed that American nuclear power has deterred the Russians and helped us survive. There is no way of proving this. It may be we survived in spite of developing a nuclear military threat.

Accident, miscalculation, and madness are ever present in any human/technological system, and this means that in the best of times there is a minimum chance that World War III will occur. And in the worst of times, such as the Cuban missile crisis, the probabilities become very high. This game of nuclear roulette aimed at Planet Earth predetermines that there will be nuclear war if the game plan continues. The question is only when. One cannot play roulette as Martin Hellman, a mathematician at Stanford points out, without the odds catching up, no matter how many times the zeroes fail to show up at first. So the current way in which we have developed "national defense" constitutes assured global genocide in the name of "defense." What is needed is real national defense in the nuclear age.

What Does De-institutionalization of War Mean?

War cannot be de-institutionalized by unilateral military reduction, or even by multilateral reduction. Such demilitarization can de-institutionalize only if these are the means, connected with other steps, toward a global goal of national defense through enforceable world law rather than national military power. Minimum requirements for a global peacekeeping system which institutionalizes peacekeeping would be:

1. A representative executive body to identify threats to the peace;

2. A representative judicial body to apply international law; and

3. A standing police force to be used as a last resort when world pressures and economic sanctions did not work.

Such a supranational structure of national defense would require that national military forces be phased out as the world system was phased in. (The detailed considerations are best analyzed in Clark and Sohn's *World Peace Through World Law.*)

What Are the Main Obstacles?

First: *structural* alternatives are rarely made visible in either educational institutions or media. Therefore, political constituencies can only ask for some form of tinkering with the pre-nuclear international system because they are only used to Band-Aid, next-step politics, not with the design and creation of a nuclear age system of enforceable world law. When there is no long-range set of system change goals, each proposal—a freeze or the elimination of a weapons system—becomes the goal instead of the means to the larger goal of the de-institutionalization of the war system.

Second: economic insecurity is a major social control instrument, so the threat of unemployment locks in the military-industrial complex. Politics to rationalize the old order follows.

So What Can Be Done?

Understanding of structural alternatives and the development of new planning politics is needed. Colleges and universities have a major responsibility to help people understand alternatives, which cannot be achieved without the extension of theory to include negative causality. Currently, most social science is descriptive and analytic, lacking even a theory of social priorities. The epistemological change from what *was* and what *is* into what *can be* and what *ought to be* permits planning of the future, and aids the realization of a major part of human nature—our inevitable role as history creators.

Politics needs to shift to long-range national (and soon global) planning goals that are ethically based, namely, to plan on the principle of "the worth and dignity of the human person." Survival in the nuclear age can then incorporate parallel social justice goals toward an ecologically sustainable economics, employment rights, and many other forms of human rights. The initial use of world law need not include more than minimum global security constitutions until people can see that law can help guarantee other human rights. In fact, there can be no human rights without world law (only human rights aspirations).

What Is Now Being Done?

Aside from the current initiatives toward reversal of the arms race, initially forced on the United States by Gorbachev's leadership, there are active NGOs such as the United Methodist Council of Bishops, The World Federalists, The Campaign for U.N. Reform, and the World Constitution and Parliament Association (see list at end of chapter).

In the 1960s, The World Law Fund (which became the Institute for World Order, then the World Policy Institute) initiated a conceptual revolution in the social sciences with "world order studies," which has been included in high school social studies.

In my own state of Oregon, I have found state Democrats willing to support a State Platform that calls for transition to the rule of law as a basis for national defense (I have copies available).

Many people have been affected by such groups as the Physicians for Social Responsibility, Educators for Social Responsibility, and Beyond War to believe that nuclear war is not survivable and that we are headed toward genocide through the current "defense" system. The dilemma for the public is that there is no basis to reject the "defense" system if no real alternative is visible. The case for the real alternative is yet to be made visible to the public. There are books, such as my own *America's Future*, which make such a case, and so the job now is to make sure that whatever influences we have are used in education and the political arena to help people understand that what has been called national defense is now obsolete, and to show that the nuclear genie can be put back in the bottle. Failure to offer structural alternatives to the war system keeps on the suicidal blinders that make us consider only technological alternatives instead of institutional transformation.

The Current Opportunities

Because the current war system not only prevents national defense but greatly inhibits economic prosperity, the opportunity to move from lose/lose to win/win provides a basis for a wide base of public support for fundamental change. College teachers of social science are the ones who have the special opportunity to educate citizens who can participate in the reconstruction of obsolete institutions and adapt institutions to people instead of people continuing to believe that economics and the international system are based on deterministic principles that are unchangeable.

Public guarantees of employment at a living wage can be realized when people understand that unemployment is part of a political game plan. Environmental depletion can be stopped when economic opportunity is based on sustainable economics. Economic development opportunities worldwide can be increased when military budgets are cut. Terrorism can be reduced when world law provides a basis for redress of grievances. But world law and the disarmament of the developed nations requires political support of the poor nations; so survival from nuclear holocaust requires empowerment of the poor and the decline of the structure of dominance.

Recent national elections in the United States have continued to be based largely on pre-nuclear conceptions of national defense and pre-ecological conceptions of economics. Those who show any real sense of these issues are considered "leftist." While those who choose lawlessness and Ramboism define the "conservative" side, thereby helping the public locate the "middle." Because we live in a new era, the definitions of "left" and "right" are obsolete.

The challenge and the opportunities for college teachers of social science have never been greater to help people achieve a better future and also to make it more likely that there be a future at all.

Organizations Working to Turn the War System into a Peacekeeping System Based on the Rule of Law

1. Parliamentarians Global Action (for disarmament, development, and world reform), 211 East 43rd Street, Suite 1604, New York, New York 10017.

2. World Policy Institute, New School University, 66 Fifth Avenue, 9th Floor, New York, New York 10011.

3. Society for Educational Reconstruction, c/o Treasurer, 6377 St. John's Drive, Eden Prairie, Miinesota 55346.

4. The Oregon Democratic Party's 1986 Foreign Policy Platform is available at PO Box 37, Sisters, Oregon 97759.

5. Citizens Global Action (an organization being developed to provide a constituency base for political candidates supporting the rule of law in international relations), 1837 SW Elm, Apt. 2, Portland, Oregon 97201.

6. World Federalists of Oregon, PO Box 19482, Portland, Oregon 97219.

7. Global Education Associates, 475 Riverside Drive, Suite 1848, New York, New York 10115.

8. American Movement for World Government, 20 West 40th Street, New York, New York 10018.

9. Campaign for U.N. Reform, 600 Valley Road, Wayne, New Jersey 17470.

10. Parliamentarians for World Order, Uganda House, 7th Floor, 336 East 45th Street, New York, New York 10017.

11. World Citizens Assembly, 312 Sutter Street, Suite 506, San Francisco, California 94108.

12. World Constitution and Parliament Assoc., 1480 Hoyt Street, Suite 31, Lakewood, Colorado 80215.

13. World Federalist Movement, 777 United Nations Plaza, 12th Floor, New York, New York 10017.

14. World Order Models Project, 495 Riverside Drive, Room 246, New York, New York 10115.

Related Books

A Common Sense Guide to World Peace, B. Ferencz (Oceana).
Toward a Human World Order, G. and P. Mische (Paulist Press).
Intro to World Peace Through World Law, Clark and Sohn (World Without War Publications).
America's Future: Transition to the 21st Century, W. H. Boyer (New Politics Publisher), PO Box 37, Sisters, OR 97759, telephone (541) 548-6544.
Let's Abolish War, T. Hudgens (BILR Corp.).

Chapter Twenty-Two

Armed Forces Ideology:
Our Mistaught GIs

*National military training
is indoctrination into the war system.
It provides anti-democratic conditioning
and is supported by the ideology
of right-wing political groups.*

Our military establishment not only teaches soldiers how to carry out military duties, but also tells them what to believe in and the social goals for which they should fight. In undertaking the latter task, it assumes a more general educational role in addition to its military training role.

Armed Forces "educational" activity of this sort is a project of vast proportions. It has millions of "students"; some of them voluntarily "attend" for the major portion of their lives, whereas others are drafted and are in compulsory attendance. The military is thus a major American educational institution—at least in scope, and possibly in influence. It behooves us to examine the extent to which this teaching reflects an official Armed Forces social philosophy (or ideology) and an official educational method.

Armed Forces material indicates that the concern for ideology was stimulated by the Korean War. American soldiers held captive in Korea often lacked adequate defense against Communist persuasion. The high mortality rate of American prisoners during that period is well known. Although the accuracy of certain military reports is being seriously challenged, it is a common (but probably false) belief that the high mortality rate resulted primarily from the ideological weakness of American soldiers. Since then the American military has focused on the problem of ideological defense; post-Korean Armed Forces publications abound with statements on "why we fight" and "what we believe."

These "why we fight" and "what we believe" articles are built on an underlying social philosophy that is often made explicit. The philosophy is commonly offered as a statement of the American way of life.

The documentation presented here must be limited, but the following quotations—samples of the views offered in official publications from 1956 to 1962—exemplify the substance of the social philosophy used by the Armed Forces. (Sources quoted here are listed at the end of this article.)

> [*Liberty is based on freedoms that are*] *God given and born in the spirit of man.*

> *The leader who thoroughly understands and exhibits moral and spiritual values will be better prepared to lead his men in this nuclear era....*

> *The foundations of liberty* [*include*] *freedom to compete in production and to bargain for goods and services in a free market.*

> [*American soldiers in Korea*] *were up against it. They couldn't answer arguments in favor of Communism with arguments in favor of Americanism....* [*They needed to know such things as:*] *Our capitalist economy is a constantly changing, flexible system. The wealth is constantly being spread on a broader base. Hundreds of thousands of steel workers, telephone operators and housewives are capitalists, owning shares of the nation's largest companies.*

> *We believe that an individual has rights, privileges and responsibilities because he is a child of God. We recognize the existence of...a basic moral law in nature. We believe that any government established by man should be based on these basic moral laws....*

The rights endowed by our creator [underlie] our American way of life.... [This pamphlet] contrasts the basic conflicts between Communism and the Free World. We as free people...believe in the true form and ideals of liberty.

These themes often recur in military literature in a consistent pattern that corresponds closely to the social philosophy variously labeled "individualism," "conservatism," or "traditional individualism." Although one of the earlier views of the basis for democratic liberty, it is only *one kind* of democratic philosophy. It presupposes that individualism and freedom are metaphysically given and therefore antecedent to social organizations and cultural experience. The individual is predefined in a combination of supernatural-capitalistic-nationalistic terms, derived mainly from Christian idealism and prescientific (natural law) realism. The view is absolutistic and leaves no room for rival democratic social philosophies. It forms an absolute separation between the complete goodness of its view and the complete evil of the only other view considered, communism. The way the problem is posed, one can select only between black and white, good and evil, or God and the devil. After this narrow stage is set, the American soldier can then use his democratic right to choose.

The choice, it seems, is determined by more than the form of the problem. Military publications commonly imply a view of the appropriate way to teach. Though they are not labeled as such, the statements refer to an educational method. Some examples:

[A recruit's] first lesson is the necessity for obedience.

Training will teach the soldier to respond from force of habit to specific battle orders....

Instill in men an aggressive attitude and desire to destroy the enemy.

[The military officer should use] reward and punishment [for] the building of good character in other individuals. [It is proper that] punishment be employed as a moral act, its prime purpose being to nourish and foster obedience.

Society has a right to...prohibit the propagation of opinions which have a dangerous tendency.... No member of society has a right to teach any doctrine contrary to what the society holds to be true.

Your purpose in carrying on a discussion with an anti-American critic is to try to change to some degree his attitude toward the U.S. and things American....

These statements indicate an educational method consistent with the absolutist features of the Armed Forces social philosophy. They approve indoctrination and a conditioning psychology. The whole fighting man—his attitudes, beliefs, concepts and habits—are considered to lie within the legitimate jurisdiction of military teaching, to be altered in the direction of military values. The method by no means fits neatly with the idea of freedom in the explicit official philosophy of traditional individualism, for it probably reflects the implicit authoritarian values of military institutions. However, the explicit adoption of both a social philosophy and an educational method establishes the Armed Forces in the role of conscious educator, whatever inconsistencies may exist between goals and methods.

A reading of Armed Forces materials produces little doubt that there is an official military social philosophy and that every effort will be used to encourage its acceptance by members of the military or any other groups the military can influence. At least two basic educational questions arise from this educational role of the Armed Forces; the first relates to *competence,* the second to *authority.*

The teachers of social philosophy in the Armed Forces are usually incompetent to teach it. That is, they are not ordinarily prepared in philosophy, education, or the social sciences and humanities. The books, pamphlets, films, and film slides that comprise the typical instructional materials are used by any officer or enlisted man who is given a leadership role. Reading materials are also available for independent study.

A pamphlet like *The Battle for Liberty* is designed as an instructor's handbook. The instructor is told how to handle questions that might arise, including a way of defending American commercial advertising. He is told how to explain the "American" view of liberty, civics, social order, education, religion, economic order, and law and order. The bibliography offers Russell Kirk, but there is no mention whatever of much more widely known writers, such as Dewey or Fromm, who expound a social philosophy at variance with that of the military.

Since no standards of academic or professional educational preparation are required to "teach" the ideology, it appears that the military relies particularly on the competence of those who prepare the material. Yet very little of the material would meet the test of scrutiny by qualified scholars. For example, its "American way of life" is not based on empirical evidence: Comparisons are made between the *actual* living conditions in Communist countries and an *idealized* version of the American way of life. The Communist threat to non-Communist countries is viewed almost entirely in military terms, and virtually no indication is given of the historical, economic, and psychological reasons underlying Communist appeal. Differences among individual Communists, among various Communist and Socialist parties, and among Communist countries are virtually ignored. And four years after the Soviet Union affirmed a policy of co-existence with the West, an official American military pamphlet said, "...there cannot be co-existence of democracy and communism, and the struggle is inevitably a mortal one."

Nor is the educational authority legitimized. Since there is no basic commitment to the canons of evidence and objectivity, Armed Forces education is neither committed to the rules of verifiable inquiry nor subject to the standards and scrutiny of professional education. Granted, professional educational organizations do not have thorough control over standards and practices in conventional institutions of public education (and, where they have some control, the standards they set are often too low), but the point is that Armed Forces teaching is wholly divorced from professional educational jurisdiction. It is, for example, entirely outside the jurisdiction of accreditation agencies. Within the normal system of standards underlying authorization of public education, the Armed Forces in its role of public educator is illicitly constituted. It is a *de facto* educational organization that fails to meet minimal educational standards of competence or to subject itself to the normal system of educational scrutiny; it therefore lacks a legitimate educational authority.

Armed Forces educational influence is not limited to servicemen. A pamphlet called *The Struggle for Men's Minds,* which includes six pictures of the Air Force ICBM, was published in 1960 for the expressed purpose of influencing public school counselors to "help students maintain ability and will to fight." The Armed Forces has its own radio stations, television programs, and publications available throughout the world. Thousands of children of military families are raised in a military environment through all their developing years.

ROTC, commonplace on college campuses, teaches military ideas through teachers who are members of the Armed Forces. Also important, though less known, are the ROTC programs in 255 public and private high schools. Two hundred and forty-one public high schools have ROTC, and forty-six have *compulsory* ROTC offered by Armed Forces personnel. A number of these students later attend a state university that compels them to take the two additional years of ROTC and they are still drafted for two full years of military service after they graduate! A number of young Americans have thus, in peacetime, received a total of *six* years of *compulsory* military "education"—no minor influence in "the struggle for men's minds."

There is no indication that military authorities consider their present educational practices to be at all questionable, nor any evidence that they disagree on the social philosophy to be taught. This is not to say that the Armed Forces is necessarily as monolithic in practice as its official ideology, but the publications give a strong impression that ideology is, officially, a closed issue rather than an area of study.

A book, *The Armed Forces Officer,* is the primary guide to the "philosophy, ideals, and principles of leadership" for officers in all branches of the military. The book suggests that the educational goals of the military are not ancillary but primary to its purpose: "Within the military establishment the inculcation of ideals is considered the most vital of all teaching."

Despite the somber, self-righteous tone of most military publications (*Military Leadership* modestly states that "the military profession has no monopoly on leadership"), they have some amusing qualities that might give them an unintentioned role as educational literature. In *The Armed Forces Officer,* the act of bringing a feudal-bureaucratic system of privilege into Twentieth-Century America without indication of conflict is a verbal spectacle that could appeal to both the logician and the gymnast. Allusions to the classics help associate an instrument of violence with the humanistic tradition in an admirable attempt to dignify the undignifiable. And tantalizing contrasts between the ideal and the real arise when the inspired assertion "than the Service, there is no other environment more conducive to the leading of the full life by the individual who is ready to accept the work of the philosopher..." is followed by an example stating that "staying with my gang meant more than anything in the world."

Possibly the most serious problem raised by Armed Forces teaching lies in its claim that the American way of life is based on one absolute American ideology which is in fundamental and irreconcilable conflict with one absolute Communist ideology. This is assumed to be the basis for the atomic arms race. Since the military establishment intentionally conveys this notion, does it not follow that it is increasing the likelihood of war by using its influence to oversimplify the problem, to narrow and thereby falsify ideological alternatives, and thus to create an irreconcilable ideological split that increases self-righteousness and hinders negotiation? What "solving" alleged absolute differences between nations with atomic weapons means should be terrifyingly obvious.

Millions of American youths have been subjected to such "education." But there is no general recognition of this fact. Since the Armed Forces in its role as educator has a far larger "enrollment" than any American school, draft policies and military personnel quotas should be recognized as having more than narrowly military significance. The decision to demand compulsory service, or even to recruit, must take into account the current educational consequences of its role as educator. And whether the military should continue its brand of education ought to be questioned, not only by professional educators, political scientists, and the like, but by the American public and by Congress.

Legitimately constituted educational organizations must take some responsibility for "professionalizing" educational services offered through public agencies, and such an interest should bring them into conflict with the present educational practices and policies of the Armed Forces. If legitimate educational organizations have a defensible basis for developing standards in those public educational institutions labeled as such, they also have a responsibility for public agencies that assume the role of educator, whether or not such agencies so call themselves. This would mean that legitimate educational organizations are responsible for getting the military either to meet the educational standards of other public educational agencies or to withdraw from its present role as educator.

For such dangerous public "education" to occur over a comparatively long period of time also raises questions about the adequacy of current American democratic processes. In our society, the military is controlled by civilians and subject to civilian scrutiny; but the actual scrutiny must indeed be feeble if the boldly displayed, officially sanctioned, ideological activities of the Armed Forces have not only failed to become a public issue but are treated as a normal part of the American way of life. The hazardous possibility is that a *means* designed to aid national defense has grown so massive and ubiquitous that it is becoming an *end* in itself—no longer simply defending a nation but increasingly characterizing it.

Sources Quoted

The Armed Forces Officer (DOD Pam 1-20), 1961.

The Battle for Liberty (DOD Pam 5-5), 1958.

John Greenway, "The Colonel's Korean 'Turncoats,'" *The Nation*, November 10, 1962.

Militant Liberty, issued through the Office of Admiral Radford, Chairman, Joint Chiefs of Staff, 1955.

Military Leadership, (FM 22-100), Department of the Army, June, 1961.

E. Paul Torrance, *The Struggle for Men's Minds*, USAF, 1960.

Chapter Twenty-Three

Teaching Peace Education through Various Subject Areas

---

*Peace studies should provide
a thoughtful basis for participating in social change.*

First, as a context for teaching peace education, one must define peace education goals, and then establish a sense of the developmental sequence so that understanding occurs in the right order.

As a definition, I propose the following: *Peace studies should provide a thoughtful basis for participating in social change by (1) focusing on alternatives to war, poverty, ecocide, and violations of human rights, and (2) designing and participating in transition toward more cooperative social systems.*

Educational Stages of Development

I. Ethical Foundations

Children need to be loved and to feel secure, and their life needs to have sufficient joy and interest so they have a basis for revering their own life and therefore life itself. Children's education needs to increase their empathy with others through cooperative action, so they have a sense of an extended self—a moral foundation for an ethically based society.

All activities have the above potential—movies, stories, care of animals, adult models, TV, peer group activities, art, and drama. But control and direction of the educational process is needed. Both permissiveness and authoritarian dominance are undesirable; one heads toward egocentric nihilism and structural anarchy, the other toward hierarchical exploitation and structural violence.

The prevention of miseducation is needed. Blind ritual designed to prevent questioning and encourage arbitrary obedience are instruments for turning children into automatons. This is exploitation in the name of education, whether by state, religion, family, or economic institution. Peace education often requires undoing ideological absolutism, racism, and other rationalizations for exploitation. Much of what is called citizenship education and religious education has been dependency indoctrination rather than humane social development.

II. Awareness of Structural Violence

Serious conflicts between nations, generations, races, sexes, and social classes can be understood through the selective use of virtually all subject areas, particularly history, sociology, political science, economics, and literature. Anthropology and social psychology has special potentialities for reducing miseducative ethnocentrism including nationalism. By the time students complete high schools, they should be able to identify the ethnocentric ideology which is transmitted through electronic media and newspapers. Their liberation from conventional mythology is a pre-requisite for the design of ethically based solutions to social conflicts.

III. Solution Education

Social problems have two solution dimensions: (1) Response to the current plight of people affected, and (2) planning the structural changes that cause and perpetuate the plight.

Description rather than problem-solving is endemic in higher education, and value judgments are so often treated as a mere point of view that a social ethics-based planning of the future has been considered heretical to the established orthodoxy. The tragic error of confusing neutrality with objectivity limits teaching and research to descriptions of what was and what is, and helps lock in the structural violence in the world by default. Solution education is based on *what was, what is, what can be, and what ought to be.* "What ought to be" should be based on what is known to be good for people—on their health, their security, their opportunity to participate in and be part of community, and on the full range of other human rights. Ethical assumptions should be not merely personal points of view but logical applications of the "worth and dignity of the human person," a dictum often stated as a cliché. Its application would consist of a radical shift in nearly all institutional and social structures, which at this period of human history are usually models of structural violence and rationalization mythology.

The most dangerous and obsolete system of structural violence is the *war system* which is rarely studied in higher education, and rarely identified in mass media. This conceptual vacuum limits political behavior to ad hoc diplomacy between nations rather than structural transformation of the war system. The academic practice of *describing* the nation-state international system, without examination of the alternatives to this war system, is the major contribution of higher education to the obliteration of the future—genocide by oversight. Peace education must give priority to the continuation of the human race. Until there is an epistemological revolution in formal education, teachers who are ready to adapt peace education objectives to their subject fields may be the pioneers in higher education who help students learn to use knowledge and information which helps them create ethics-centered social systems.

Examples

Philosophy teachers could help students understand the difference between absolutistic truth and universal values as a basis for exploring the a priori ethical basis for human rights.

History teachers could encourage students to explore what might have been instituted in the international system prior to a particular war in order to have prevented it.

Literature classes could use novels that show the suffering of people affected by obsolete political structures, such as John Hershey's *Hiroshima* or Steinbeck's *Grapes of Wrath*.

Science programs could tie chemistry and physics into biology and ecology to gain insight in the nature of the life support system, as a basis for understanding current threats to the biosphere.

Physical education programs could use games that are enjoyable and body-building, but not cruel and crippling. Students could invent rules for games to help them see that all rules are social inventions.

Economics classes should help students evaluate economic alternatives on the basis of economic justice, common quality of life, and ecological sustainability instead of ethnocentric ideology.

Political science should help students examine how public policy can contribute to the elimination of poverty, war, and ecocide as obsolete institutions caused by the lack of the appropriate application of political power.

Anthropology should help students avoid the belief that each culture has self-justifying standards by developing standards for the evaluation of culture based on human rights.

Professional schools should educate professionals to serve social needs instead of dominant economic interests.

Institutions of higher education should be guided by social priorities, and faculty should participate in giving such direction to their institutions. Those who work with peace education theory should be particularly able to provide such direction, for the ethical foundations of peace education and its emphasis on citizenship are what is needed to give responsible direction to the entire higher education enterprise.

Chapter Twenty-Four

Olsolete U. S. Policies Fail To Deter Global Terrorism

> *Continuation of American world dominance*
> *will not provide security for Americans.*
> *Control of third world nations*
> *produces reaction including terrorism.*

Terrorism produces understandable frustration, and people have little preparation to understand such bizarre acts except to label the perpetrators as mad dogs and to strike back with a big fist.

However attractive it is to have a simplistic explanation and a scapegoat, the widespread approval of such acts as the military bombing of Libya may be as terrifying as the terrorism itself, for when people uncritically rally to the flag in the nuclear age they may unintentionally be part of the process which can lead to nuclear war, the ultimate terrorism.

Many people who are polled and supportive of the bombing have been raised on the messages of *The Empire Strikes Back, Rambo,* and similar genre. Their frustrations may be temporarily assuaged by unleashing the Pentagon, believing that we "taught them a lesson" or, as Oregonian headlines said, that the bombing of Libya was a "success."

Exactly what did we succeed in doing? Will terrorists not only in Libya but in Syria, Iran, and Lebanon cringe and say, "Please stop it; we won't do it again?" No chance.

The world's most powerful nation, deemed imperialist by most third-world nations, has chosen unilateral intervention with bombers to "send a message." Unlike a Western Union message, the interpretation is based on the eye of the beholder—that America is frustrated and doesn't know what else to do. President Ronald Reagan sought to rally-around-the-flag during an election year, but the allies didn't share Reagan's military orientation, so he had to go it alone. The United States was not interested in multilateral approaches to military threat and desperately tried to preserve the fading American dominance.

The message we sent by lobbing 16-inch shells into Lebanese villages was a rousing success, at least with respect to the recruitment of young religious fundamentalists whose life now has purpose— produce terrorism against Americans. Will those whose families were injured or killed in Tripoli be also offered a lifelong purpose? Who is now ready to buy airline tickets to the new "pacified" Europe?

We hear nothing from the administration about basic causes of Mideast terrorism, yet it is clear that most of it stems from failure to resolve the Palestinian issue, and when Israel is embraced by the United States and the Arabs are ignored—except when they control oil—the prospects for an American contribution to a peaceful solution are not high.

Even with good intentions, a single Western nation is not likely to resolve the issue, though the Carter administration made a first-rate try. The complex injustices and threats to international peace require multilateral action including use of the World Court rather than acts such as mining the harbors of Nicaragua.

Should our government's credibility and claim to irrefutable facts be accepted at face value? President Lyndon B. Johnson manipulated the truth about the Gulf of Tonkin "attack" in order to justify bombing of North Vietnam, and the Reagan administration claimed "certain and irrefutable proof" that the Russians were engaged in chemical warfare with "yellow rain" in Southeast Asia, until the material was sent to Harvard and scientists found it to be bee droppings.

So if a "confirmed" Khadafy-sponsored plan to bomb a Berlin disco is not a sufficient basis for open military warfare on Libya, is the allegation even true? With a president anxious to attack Khadafy and with his proven willingness to be the great prevaricator whenever it is useful (i.e., Navy maneuvers in the Gulf of Syria were "just routine"), why should our allies, or the public, or Congress be willing to accept the Berlin evidence as irrefutable? Why not ask what we teach high school social studies students: What is the real evidence?

But terrorism as a serious issue is very real and solutions are needed. They require action, however, at different levels. One level requires specific police action to intercept and deter terrorists and to try them as the murderers they are.

The other level requires attention to underlying terrorist goals, for most terrorism is politics by other means. As long as the world has no formal structures such as world law for adjudicating claims of nations or groups, the remaining choices define the forms of actions that are available. Weaker nations or groups are most likely to resort to suitcase explosives to attract attention and change behavior, if they are sufficiently desperate and sufficiently frustrated.

Big nations can mine harbors, parade navies and missiles, invade smaller nations, or even threaten global genocide and nuclear winter, carefully trying to avoid being labeled superterrorists merely because they behave as normal superpowers.

Structural transformation of the international system toward diminished terrorism at all levels requires more multilateral cooperation between nations, but it especially requires the development of enforceable world law so that dispute settlement can occur the way it does within nations, through the nonviolent arena of enforceable law. Such law needs to have a high level of public respect to make it work, but if it serves a wide range of interests it has the basis for worldwide support. As world law provides better solutions than terrorism, the terrorists—whether they are Palestinians, Contras, or whatever—will lose their support status as "heroes" and "freedom fighters" and will become known as outlaws and threats to world peace.

The prevention of nuclear war and the reduction of small-scale terrorism both depend on moving from an international hierarchy of dominance based on the threat of violence to the rule of law based on fair and enforceable principles, many of which are contained in current international law.

Recent and current administrations head consistently in the wrong direction, flouting international law and the World Court and trying to use military dominance rather than cooperative world community based on world law as a basis for international dispute settlement.

It is tragic but not surprising that Americans are likely to be the preferred terrorist targets. It is also tragic, but not necessary, for Americans to embrace obsolete politics of national dominance which move us toward a world where threat and violence escalate and where no hopeful future is possible.

Section Four

Glossary
and
Sources

Chapter Twenty-Five

A Transition Glossary

*This new era in human history requires
some new concepts and definitions.*

The terms presented here are organized under seven headings: *Biological Ecology, Human Population, Resources, Pollution, Values, Systems,* and *Planning.*

Biological Ecology

The interdependence of organisms, including people, with each other and with their physical environment.

Term	*Concept*
Biological control	The introduction of birds, animals, insects, or fish to control other organisms.
Community	The populations of all species that live in a particular area.

Cycles: water, CO_2, carbon, nitrogen, phosphorus	Natural recycling systems of movement through an ecosystem, often through plants and animals activated by solar energy. The water cycle, for example, includes evaporation, rain, rivers, and ocean.
Decomposers	Organisms such as worms, bacteria, and fungi that eat dead organic material and convert it into nutrients.
Diversity	The complexity of a community.
Dominance	Control by a plant or animal of the largest portion of energy in a community.
Ecological niche	The unique function of a plant or animal in a biological community; its place in the ecological system.
Endangered species	Plants, animals, fish, birds, or insect species that are being destroyed so rapidly that without better protection they may cease to exist.
Entropy	The loss of energy during energy transfer. All transfer in the food web involves entropy (the second law of thermodynamics).
Food webs	Interdependent feeding levels which involve transfer of energy and materials.
Nitrogen-fixing bacteria	Soil bacteria that convert inorganic nitrogen into usable plant nutrients.
Photosynthesis	The process by which green plants convert solar energy into chemical energy.

Plankton	Microscopic plants and animals found in lakes, rivers, and oceans; they are at the beginning of the food chain.
Symbiosis	An association of dissimilar organisms, producing mutual benefits.
Territoriality	A sense of possession of an area, which the possessor defends against intruders.
Watershed	A land area that catches rain and guides it above ground and underground into a common outlet.

Human Population

The numbers of people in any human community.

Term	*Concept*
Contraceptive	Mechanical, surgical, or chemical means of preventing pregnancy.
Doubling time	The time it takes for a population to double.
Exponential increase	Geometrical increase in population that accelerates the total numbers through doubling times: 1, 2, 4, 8, 16, 32, 64, etc.
Family planning	Having only the number of children per family that is desired by the husband and wife.
Population age distributions	The proportional numbers at various age levels. Countries differ in their distribution patterns.

Population mobility   Movements of people from one area to another, either in large numbers or continuous flows.

Zero population growth   Having only the number of births that replace deaths, so that the total population does not increase.

Resources

Natural and human materials and processes which people might use to serve human objectives. For example, resources can include minerals, food, and information.

Term	Concept
Energy	Capacity to do work. Work produces change but requires power. Energy makes plants grow, wind blow, and automobiles go. It permits us to think and move. Energy sources can come from stored fossil fuel, incoming solar energy, geothermal heat, tides, and fission and fusion nuclear sources.
Nonrenewable	Resources that are finite in amount, such as petroleum or minerals, and cannot be replaced if they are consumed or destroyed.
Nutrients	The chemical and biological elements that provide energy and growth to plants and animals.
Renewable	Resources that can be replaced when consumed or destroyed, such as wheat or fish.

Pollution

Contamination that reaches levels destructive to the maintenance of the quality of the life-support system.

Term	Concept
Pollution	Pollution can occur in air, water, land, and food and may be experienced through human senses.
Eutrophication	Pollution can occur through *eutrophication,* which speeds up growth in water and fills in lakes and rivers with plants and sedimentation.
Toxification	Pollution can occur through *toxification,* which either kills or injures the organism. For instance, automobile exhaust produces toxic pollution that makes "smog" which contributes to discomfort, illness, and death.

Values

Judgments of worth or desirability.

Term	Concept
Cooperation	People working together for the good of the group.
Democracy	Participation by members of a group in the formation of group rules and politics.
Equity	A fair distribution of the goods, services, and opportunities generated by an economic system.

Esthetic value	The quality of an experience, not instrumental to something else, but "good" in itself. Esthetic value combines understanding and feeling and can consist of the beauty of art, nature, or the style and quality of human behavior.
Ethical values	"The worth and dignity of the human person," applied to an assessment of human consequences of human actions. Ethical values can operate through direct interpersonal relations and also through indirect institutional action such as government, economics, and business.
Health	A state in which disease is absent, resistance to disease is high, and the body functions properly at a level of abundant energy.
Progress	A set of social changes seen as providing a better life for most of a society's members.
Quality of life	Environmental, social, and personal characteristics that contribute to the desirability of one's life.
Social ethics	The service of public values through the explicit social goals of political, economic, or institutional structures.

Systems

A set of interdependent parts where the whole is greater than the sum of its parts. There are *natural* physical and biological systems, *social* systems such as economic systems, and *technological* systems such as a highway system. Natural systems are created by nature; social and technical systems are invented by people.

Term	*Concept*
An ecocide system	A system in which political and economic rules determine that there will be progressive deterioration of the ecological life-support system.
A poverty system	A system in which political and economic rules determine that poverty will be the outcome.
A war system	A system in which anarchy and national sovereignty are the rules of international organization, and military violence instead of law is the instrument for the ultimate resolution of international conflict.
Closed system	A system with finite and fixed number of parts. Nonrenewable resources are part of a "closed system."
Open system	A system with expanding number of parts. Symbolic systems can be "open." Ideas and information can be increased without exhausting the supply.
Growth system	Commonly used to mean the quantitative expansion of an economy which increases wages, profits, gross national product, and the amount of goods and services.
Interdependence	A system in which members rely on each other for their mutual benefit.
Life-support system	The air, soil, water, and heat on the surface of the earth that provide a basis for organisms and human life to survive through the development of ecological systems.

Malthusian	Referring to the theory of Thomas Malthus, an Eighteenth-Century economist, who saw that if population expands geometrically while food expands at a slower rate, people would soon starve. The concept now refers to the dire consequences of permitting open expansion of population and consumption in a life-support system with limited resources.
No-growth system	A stagnant economic system that does not change significantly.
Steady-state system	A society and its economy in a state of ecological equilibrium which is able to keep the life-support system from deteriorating. A *dynamic* steady-state system reorganizes the economy to improve quality of life while also achieving ecological equilibrium.
Structural exploitation	The exploitation produced when a social system (poverty, ecocide, political, economic, or institutional) takes unfair advantage over some to provide advantages to others.
Structural murder	The destruction of human life by social systems such as the war system, the poverty system, and the ecocide system, which predetermine that unnecessary death will occur.
Structural violence	Violence produced by a social system (war, poverty, ecocide; political, economic, or institutional) because of the very nature of that system.

Supranational	Operating on a political level higher than national law or politics. World law or world government would be supranational.
Transnational	Extending beyond national identity. Religious and scientific groups can be transnational when they are not attached to national loyalties.
Tragedy of the commons	A parable environmentalists use to show how individual interests in exploiting natural resources contradict the survival needs of the community. If the common life-support system has finite resources, a procedure that permits individuals to use more than their fair share will cause destruction to the "commons." The commons can be land or any other limited resource.

Planning

Planning can be individual or social. It is a process used to decide on the best goals and the best means to achieve those goals. Social planning of cities and countries tries to reduce human dependence on random accidents and to permit common goals to be achieved and the future to be more predictable. City planning is now a common practice.

Term	Concept
Ad hoc	Piecemeal planning that responds with short-range solutions to separate problems.
Carrying capacity	The maximum capacity of an area to support a given population without destruction of the life-support system or the quality of life.

Cost/Benefit Analysis	Procedures for assessing whether there is more to be gained than to be lost by a plan. Cost/benefit analysis can include economic, social, and ecological considerations.
Environmental Impact Statement (E.I.S.)	An attempt to predict impacts on environment and may apply a cost/benefit analysis to a specific proposed project.
External costs	The cost paid by the larger society rather than by the manufacturer. For instance, there may be costs which a manufacturer pays to have garbage taken away, but the larger society may pay for the costs of the garbage dump, the pollution of ground water, and the loss of the resources in the garbage. The social cost can be in money, health, and quality of life.
Forecasting	Using scientific methods to anticipate the future; often involves projecting trends such as population increases to see where they are heading. Permits decisions on whether to change trends or adapt to them.
Futuristics	The study of the kinds of futures that are possible; it provides a basis for deciding which is the most desirable.
Integrative	Planning that takes account of a number of problems and goals simultaneously and aims toward both short- and long-range solutions.
Involuntary suicide	Killing oneself inadvertently because of lack of knowledge, such as of pollution or nutrition.

Irreversibility	Refers to an action or condition which prevents a second chance, such as when petroleum is burned or prime topsoil is lost to the point at which erosion or desert replaces a stable, productive ecosystem.
Lead time	The advance time it will take to develop a plan and put it into effect. Major changes in energy sources may take decades, e.g., shifting from one system (petroleum) to another (solar, etc.). Therefore, forecasting is necessary to anticipate the lead time.
Low-energy consumption technology	Machines and other kinds of technology which are designed to use minimum amounts of energy, such as a small car vs. a big car.
Overload	Exceeding carrying capacity.
Participatory planning	Democratic involvement by the community in the planning process.
Pesticides	Chemical technology for insect control. Specific pesticides kill a precise group of insects; broad-spectrum pesticides kill a great number of types of insects.
Political design	The establishment of a common future to be realized and of public policies and implementation to bring that future into being.
Priorities	Decisions that provide an order of importance for a number of planning objectives.

Trade-off

A decision (based on priorities) concerning what should be given up in order to achieve something else. Trade-offs are necessary when two objectives cannot both be achieved without some sacrifice of one or both objectives.

Voluntary suicide

Killing oneself directly or indirectly through actions such as smoking, driving fast, or eating injurious foods, even though one understands the consequences.

Zero-sum vs. nonzero-sum

When scarce resources are divided among a limited number of people, the more some get, the less others get. If some win, others lose. Zero-sum applies to scarce resources and raises the question of equitable distribution. Zero-sum applies also to future generations. The petroleum used now is taken from future generations. In nonzero sum, abundant resources are created so no one has to lose what another gains.

Original Sources of Articles:
Permissions Granted

Section One

Chapter One first appeared as: William Boyer, "Old Order/ New Order," *SER in ACTION,* Summer 1997, Volume 8, Number 3, pp. 9-10, 23.

Chapter Two first appeared as: William Boyer, "Creativity Type II, Designing and Creating World Futures," *McGill Journal of Education,* 1973, Volume VIII, Number 1, pp. 73-85.

Chapter Three first appeared as: William Boyer, "Education for Survival," *Phi Delta Kappan,* January 1971, pp. 258-262.

Chapter Four first appeared as: William Boyer, "Reconstructive Versus Expansive Planning," pp. 229-321 in Nobuo Shimahara (editor), *Educational Reconstruction,* Chas. Merrill, 1973.

Chapter Five first appeared as: William Boyer, "Planning Education and Systems Change," *The Educational Forum,* May 1973, pp. 391-401.

Chapter Six first appeared as: William Boyer, "Universities and Social Priorities," *Prioritas,* February 1978, pp. 13-17.

Chapter Seven first appeared as: William Boyer, "Reconstructing Social Science," paper delivered at the 1989 Meeting of the Oregon Peace Studies Consortium.

Chapter Eight first appeared as: William Boyer, "Toward an

Ecological Perspective in Education," *Phi Delta Kappan,* February 1974, pp. 397-399.

Chapter Nine first appeared as: William Boyer, "Environmental Rights: Legal Standing for Future Generations," paper presented at the XV World Conference of the World Futures Studies Federation, Brisbane, Australia, September 1997.

Chapter Ten first appeared as: William Boyer, "Electing the Future," paper presented at the World Meeting of the Futures Studies Federation, Hungary, May 1990

Section Two

Chapter Eleven first appeared as: William Boyer & Paul Walsh, "Are Children Born Unequal?" *Saturday Review,* October 19, 1969, pp. 63-79.

Chapter Twelve first appeared as: William Boyer, "Have Our Schools Kept Us Free?" *The School Review,* Volume 71, Number 2, 1963, pp. 222-228.

Chapter Thirteen first appeared as: William Boyer, "Oversight in Value Education," *The Third Yearbook of the Arizona Association for Supervision and Curriculum Development,* 1975, pp. 11-19.

Chapter Fourteen first appeared as: William Boyer, "Teaching Capitalist Economics in Public Schools," *Clearing House,* December 1979.

Chapter Fifteen first appeared as: William Boyer, "Economic Miseducation," *Educational Perspectives,* November 17, Number 2, May 1978, pp. 30-32.

Section Three

Chapter Sixteen first appeared as: William Boyer, "Defining Peace Studies," *COPRED Peace Chronicle,* August 1987, pp. 13-15.

Chapter Seventeen first appeared as: William Boyer, "War Education," *Phi Delta Kappan,* May 1967, pp. 418-421.

Chapter Eighteen appeared as: William Boyer, "Junior ROTC: Militarism in the Schools," *Phi Delta Kappan,* November 1964, pp. 117-122.

Chapter Nineteen first appeared as: William Boyer, "Misunderstanding Defense," *Honolulu Star-Bulletin,* July 10, 1982.

Chapter Twenty first appeared as: William Boyer, "World Order Education: What is It?," *Phi Delta Kappan,* April 1975, pp. 514-522.

Chapter Twenty-One first appeared as: William Boyer, "The De-Institutionalization of War," paper presented at the Western Social Science Association, 1987.

Chapter Twenty-Two first appeared as: William Boyer, "Armed Forces Ideology: Our Mistaught GIs," *The Nation,* November 30, 1963.

Chapter Twenty-Three first appeared as: William Boyer, "Teaching Peace Education Through Various Subject Areas," unpublished instructional guide.

Chapter Twenty-Four first appeared as: William Boyer, "Obsolete U.S. Politics Fail To Deter Global Terrorism," *Vanguard.*

Section Four

Chapter Twenty-Five first appeared as: William Boyer, "Transition Glossary," in William Boyer, *America's Future, Transition to the 21st Century, New Politics,* 1984, pp. 155-163.

About the Author

William Boyer is professor emeritus in philosophy of education at the University of Hawaii. He has a B.A. degree in philosophy from the University of Oregon, a Masters degree in the teaching of English from the University of Colorado, a doctorate in philosophy of education from Arizona State University, and post-doctoral study at Stanford University.

He first taught in high school, then at the University of Oregon, Portland State University, the University of Montana, and Oregon State University, prior to the University of Hawaii. He introduced new areas of environmental education, future studies, long range planning, and war prevention education. He was in the Air Force in World War II and in the democratization program in Germany after the war.

He has been an activist and community organizer in forest

conservation and land use planning and created a movement for providing legal rights to future generation. His publications include three previous books—*Education for Annihilation*, *Alternative Futures: Designing Social Change*, and *America's Future: Transition to the 21st Century*—published by Praeger and Greenwood.

Professor Boyer can be contacted at Box 37, Sisters, Oregon 97759.